Stop Recruiting
Start Attracting

A Book About
Change and Membership
In Rotary Clubs

Dr. Bill Wittich

ISBN # ISBN: 978-0-988270-1-1

*Knowledge Transfer Publishing
8650 Heritage Hill Drive
Elk Grove, CA 95624
916-601-2485
billwittich@comcast.net
www.volunteerpro.net*

First Edition

About the Author

Dr. Bill Wittich is a speaker, consultant, and author in the field of leadership, motivation, and nonprofit management.

For the past twelve years, Bill and his wife Ann have traveled an average of 200 days a year. Their speaking schedule has taken them to all corners of the United States and through much of Europe.

His doctorate is from the University of Southern California where he continues to serve as a mentor to graduate students in the School of Policy, Planning, and Development.

Dr. Wittich has authored seven books in the association and non-profit field.

He is Past President of the Rotary Club of Laguna Sunrise in Elk Grove, California and he serves as an Assistant Governor for District 5180. He is an instructor for membership at the Far West President-Elect Training Seminars.

They enjoy living in Elk Grove, where they enjoy cooking, collecting antiques, and learning about red wine.

Other Publications
By Dr. Bill Wittich

The Care and Feeding of Volunteers

Model Volunteer Handbook

A Collection of Volunteer Forms

Celebrate Differences

77 Ways to Recruit Volunteers

77 Ways to Recognize Volunteers

Keep Those Volunteer Around

Energize Your Rotary Club

Attract the Best Volunteers

"Long term, strong clubs are the answer to Rotary's membership challenge. Clubs that are diverse in age, gender and ethnicity. These are the clubs that attract and retain members. Bill's new book gives us the path to stronger clubs."

Don Kremer, Rotary Coordinator, Zone 26, 2010-2013

"Dr. Bill Wittich makes us realize in his new book that we must first make our club attractive to others before they will want to become a member of our club."

David Gallagher, District 5220 Centennial Governor

"Once again Dr. Wittich puts it right up front and personal: There is relief for membership malaise, but the collective WE must make it work."

Bill Short, Governor 2013-2014, District 5180

"Bill Wittich knows his Rotary very well indeed. And he seems to understand the art of motivating volunteerism far better than most of us. This book speaks clearly and simply about making Rotary attractive to its prospects

Dave Cresson, Coordinator, Rotary Public Image Resource Group

"Bill understands the membership challenges facing Rotary and explores innovative ways to attract our new generation of Rotarians."

Phillip Sammer, District Governor, District 5000, Hawaii

This book is dedicated to all the World-Class Rotarians

I've met in my life who continue to inspire me

Introduction

This is a book about membership and change. Maybe it is about change and then membership. Change is hard for everyone, but very difficult for Rotary clubs. John Kotter in an article on change in the Harvard Business Review said that 70% of change efforts fail to achieve their desired goal. Wow! Should we bother? My answer is that Rotary is usually in that other 30 percent that gets things done. Think about Polio Plus or the Peace Forums or clean water around the world. Rotary can make change happen. But change in our clubs has been a slow movement.

Yes, this book is about Change and Membership.

Club leaders have the ability to build a nimble team that is engaged and focused on continually getting better. They can see their clubs grow, expand and build better communities.

Membership is a critical change area for all service clubs. It is critical to continue to add new members, because each year members will leave for a variety of reasons. They move away, they pass away, they lose their interest, they run out of money, and they disagree with the way the club is going. It does not really matter why they leave, it is important to find new people to replace those who leave. Too many clubs spend months thinking about how to recruit new members into their club. It is more important to find out how to attract members into your club.

If your club is not attractive to a number of people in your community, you might as well stop recruiting. Attraction must come first. This is a major change for clubs to move from an older view of recruitment to a new area of building attraction.

Wikipedia tells us that attraction means the drawing of one object towards another. In Rotary it means drawing one person toward a Rotary club.

The question we need to deal with in this book is how do we entice guests to visit our club and not only come back but convert them into committed and dedicated Rotarians.

We will need to decide exactly who we want to attract into our club and why. We know that our current RI President Ron Burton is telling us to be engaging and if we engage our guests will it help them to decide to join. Maybe Seth Godin has it right in his book *Tribes* when he says that a tribe is a group of people connected to one another, connected to a leader, and connected to an idea. Godin says that "Tribes need leadership, they need connection and growth and something new." They need change. His major theme in the book rings with me. That is "You can't have a tribe without a leader and you can't be a leader without a tribe." Is he talking about Rotary? I think so. Where is a strong club without a strong leader? And where is a strong leader without a club?

Maybe this book is about change, membership and being a strong leader with a tribe.

Rotary International President Ron Burton said it so well. "We're not asking just anyone to join Rotary. We're looking to attract busy, successful, motivated people who care." The key thought from President Ron is that we are not looking to recruit warm bodies; we are looking to attract the right people into Rotary. Attracting the right people means you must put together a program that will help to locate these people. In the corporate world, we call that marketing. In the Rotary world, we call that Public image.

You have to build your marketing first before anyone even knows you exist.

Marketing is a tool used to build attraction in your club. Public image allows people to see what the Rotary club offers even before they see themselves in it. Marketing in the past meant putting articles in your local newspaper. Today it means using various forms of social media to gain the eyes of those prospective members.

Your audience needs to know that you are in their community. Prospective members either live or work in your community and in either case they need to know that you are there. It is true that you need to invite people to visit your club, but unless they are aware of all the good things your club does, it will be more difficult.

Today many Rotary clubs are not effective in attracting members into their fold. Their membership numbers have not changed over the past year with the exception that they may have lost a few members. You visit the typical club and you see the mix of middle-aged and older members. They may have

added a few women and ethnic members to their roster but not many younger members. This book will
explore how clubs can be successful in growing their
membership. I think most of us will agree that if Rotary is to remain a strong service club then we must
continue to add new members.

These new members must include a mix of younger,
middle aged and older members. It must include
gender and ethnic diversity as well. It is this variety
in membership that increases the quality of a club's
membership.

Mark Levin in *Millennium Membership* says it so well,
"It's not your father's (or Mother's) organization anymore." He explains that only the clubs that understand the value of adding diversity will succeed in
attracting members of any age.

This means that clubs may need to change their
membership process. It is critical for all Rotary leaders to understand that what brought them into

Rotary may not be the same thing that will bring this next member into Rotary. Rotary International is making a number of changes, but many club members are not paying attention to these changes. Or, even worse, they may be fighting these changes and trying so hard to maintain the status quo.

It may not even be the idea of change; it may be the speed of this change.

We will discuss these changes and offer suggestions for helping clubs adjust and understand what it will take to find new members.

We must think about change, not only the changes in the Rotary organization, but the changes occurring today in the lives of our members. We must be aware that technology is changing everything about Rotary. My District meetings are held these days

through *Go-To-Meeting*, where we all connect
through our computers.

This saves time and allows us to stay off the road allowing our busy members more time for work and
family. My point is that technology has already
changed much about Rotary membership and club
operations.

The goal of this book is to understand what their
members expect and how to offer it to them. It is critical to understand your prospective member's views,
if we are to attract them into Rotary. We need to see
what is going on in their lives, both their personal,
family and Rotary lives. By understanding all three
parts, it will help us to see how it affects their view of
Rotary membership.

*Your club needs to invest
in technology and use it to attract
new members.*

Technology such as websites, blogs, Facebook and Twitter are no longer an option, they are a given.

Rotary clubs must be at the forefront of social media to attract new members, particularly younger members. Just take a look around Starbucks and watch those young professionals interacting with their smart phones, tablets and computers. These tools are their networking lives and Rotary needs to fit into this arena.

The fresh perspective and out-of-the-box thinking that younger members can bring may open new avenues for your club. Through this, younger members may be able to bring a new network of younger members that will be the future for carrying out your Rotary mission. While young people can often be counted on to know what is new and hot in the technology world, they can bring more to the table than just being able to set up the LCD projector with ease. Many young people are enthusiastic fundraisers, marketing whizzes, financial geniuses, and special-events gurus.

While the current excitement is finding young people to bring into Rotary, there may well be another group of prospects that we might focus on. Those are that large group of retiring Boomers that could help to increase our membership. These Boomers are retiring at the rate of 10,000 of them each day for the next decade. They are a vital group of healthy, wealthy and wise potential Rotarians that we may overlook if we are not aware of them. They are very different from those young prospects in many ways and the attraction process is different for both groups.

You may wonder why I am not looking at those in-between ages, those prospects between the ages of 40 and 65. I am certainly interested in bringing them on board, but in many cases they are already our members and are leading our clubs today. I see this group of 50 year olds at the President Elect Training Seminars preparing to take the reins of their clubs.

But I hope that this book will convince you that all generations are needed for Rotary to continue its drive to the future. It is just that my focus will be on these two primary areas of focus, the younger ones and those Baby Boomers, and hopefully you will agree with me or at least give me a chance to convince you of the value of your focus on these two generations.

One thing that both the younger and the Boomer generations have is endless energy

This is energy that they are looking to throw into a cause that they care about, or that will further their professional careers or retirement days. Incorporating both generations into your club can add this much needed shot of energy and foster new, different, and progressive ideas that can reenergize the club. If you expect the best from a young member, you will get it. If you expect that the new Boomer members will give their all, you are right. I believe all Rotarians are in agreement that we need to attract new members into our clubs. Let's get started by thinking about why we are concerned with member-ship.

All Service Clubs are in Trouble

While all service clubs are losing members for a number of reasons, the nation's three largest, Rotary, Lions, and Kiwanis are losing the most members. But we are most concerned about Rotary's loss in membership. Rotary membership in North America dropped from its peak of 445,434 in 1996 to 341,951 in 2013.

Lisa Johnson in *Mind Your X's and Ys* says that traditional social groups, including Rotary, Elks, and chambers of commerce are struggling to maintain membership. But service clubs are not alone, according to the latest Member Marketing Benchmark Report; over half of the professional associations in the United States are experiencing a decline in membership.

It appears that the tough economy, too many competing organizations, and all those Internet resources are making it harder to attract members. "In previous generations, the only way to network was to join a professional organization, but now a lot of the benefits that someone gets socially can be achieved online," says Lauren Hefner, director of membership for the Virginia-based Laboratory Products Association. "We're a lot less likely to do something in person that we can do online without having to travel or spend money."

Service clubs are fighting a variety of challenges.

Their members are growing older and very few young people are signing up to take their place. The clubs also are having a hard time getting the public to understand just what it is that service clubs do. "I think the biggest misconception people have about service clubs is that we're a bunch of old guys getting together to eat," said Rotarian Marty Wood of Linwood, Washington. "We have to get the understanding out there that we do good things in the community."

The current economy may be one issue for this declining membership, but there appear to be many other reasons for this loss. But the economy is certainly an issue for many current and potential members.

In *Bowling Alone*, Robert Putnam makes a powerful argument that in the last several decades of the twentieth century, all sorts of community groups and in particular, service clubs have begun to fade. Putnam states that ... " It wasn't so much that old members dropped out, at least not anymore rapidly than age and the accidents of life had always meant. But community organizations were no longer continuously revitalized, as they had been in the past, by freshets of new members."

You may wonder why this freshet does not include those up and coming young professionals in your community. It might be that many of your younger professionals do not even know what a service club is or what it does. This may be because we fail to market our clubs to these younger prospects. We do not talk about Rotary at college business classes or at chambers of commerce.

Most clubs have not worked on starting a Rotaract club at the local college or an Interact club in the high school. Rotaract is a Rotary-sponsored service club for young men and women ages 18 to 30. Rotaract clubs are either community or college based, and are sponsored by a local Rotary club. Rotaract clubs are a perfect avenue to attract younger members to Rotary clubs. Once these Rotaractors graduate and enter the work force, they will be ready for full Rotary membership.

The word Interact stands for "international action," and today nearly 200,000 high school students in more than 110 countries belong to some 8,700 clubs.

This is making Interact a truly international phenomenon.

All over the world, young people are spreading fellowship and international understanding through a wide array of Interact service activities. All Interact clubs undertake service activities that teach leadership skills, allow the students to serve their community, and help expand international understanding. But the question remains, how many of these young Interactors ever end up as Rotary members? Do our clubs work to find and attract them into membership? The answer in most cases is no, which we do not tend to track either Rotaractors or Interactors once they graduate and move into the work world.

According to a *Report on the Recruitment of Rotary Alumni as Prospective Rotarians,* "These Rotaract and Interact programs not only attract the best and brightest young people, they also produce individuals with a commitment to leadership, service, and international understanding."

The individuals who participate in these programs become contributing members of their communities and share the values they learned in Rotary with the rest of the world. Because of their dedication to Rotary's values, it seems that these program alumni would make great Rotarians. They are already more familiar with Rotary than the average prospective member and their participation in Rotary's programs indicates that they are interested in Rotary's objectives. The question from Rotary International is "Why not capitalize on their previous experience with Rotary and get a return on the investment by keeping them involved in Rotary as a member?" Yet for some reason it appears that majorities of Rotary clubs do not recruit these alumni for membership. The alumni themselves will tell you that their exposure to Rotary through their program has a significant impact on their desire to join.

But the fact remains that most clubs tend to ignore these alumni after they finish their program.

It isn't that young people are not volunteering, said sociologist Peter Levine, of the Center for Information and Research on Civic Learning and Engagement at Tufts University. They just do not tend to join organizations such as Rotary, which can require weekly meetings at restaurants; and the time commitment of serving on committees. Instead, young people and parents of young children volunteer for events and charities that they can fit into busy work and family lives. Over fifty percent of all US teens volunteer and the teen volunteering rate is twice the adult volunteering rate of 29 percent. If we can get these teens thinking about Rotary, we can continue this high volunteering rate and add to our membership.

A Loss of Members

Even as membership is dropping in Rotary clubs in North America, the number of Rotary clubs is growing slightly. Back in 1994 there were 8700 Rotary clubs in North America, but now, there are 8791 clubs. Even as we charter new clubs, we are still facing a serious loss of members.

Rotary requires that a club have a minimum of twenty members to charter. But many clubs drop down to a much smaller number of members than that before Rotary considers pulling their charter.

One major concern is just how few members you allow a club to have and how this small size might effect the recruiting of new members.

There appears to be a "magic" number of members for a club to function well. We simply do not know this "magic" number. It appears to differ club by club. What we do know is that Rotary clubs take on community service projects and that requires a significant number of members. A loss of members might mean taking on less service projects or at least slowing down this rate of service.

Since one of the main reasons members join a service club is to perform community service, less service projects might lead to retention problems. As many members get older they start thinking about writing a check rather than do that hands-on community service that is the "Service Above Self" theme of Rotary. Don't misunderstand me, checks and credit cards bring in needed funds for club projects, but Rotary has always been a hands-on service organization.

Younger people are already volunteering in large numbers at schools and for local community service projects. But Rotary clubs are not seeing the result of this service. These young people are not working with the local Rotary club. It might be that the younger people in the community are volunteering with their church and youth activities.

Very likely even the younger professionals are joining other organizations that are aimed at younger professionals.

An example of this is a program of the Sacramento Metro Chamber called Metro EDGE. It represents more than 500 of the Sacramento region's young professionals from a myriad of business sectors, ethic groups and education levels. They stress that these are the "tech-savvy social-media mavens who are green-conscious entrepreneurs." Their goal is to "engage, develop, and empower the 40-and-under young leaders of the Sacramento region."

Their definition of a young professional includes highly entrepreneurial, civic-minded people between the ages of 21 and 40 with a college degree. Metro EDGE tells us that young professionals represent nearly 25 percent of the downtown population in large metro areas. Are these not the exact group that Rotary is looking to attract into clubs?

 Even more scary is the exact comments from the chair of Metro EDGE Ryan Porter concerning their vision for attracting these young professionals. " We will focus on building our region from within by engaging, developing and empowering our young professionals while giving back to the community as a whole." Does this not sound like the Rotary vision?

Why is Rotary not recruiting these same young professionals? Why are these young professionals not considering local Rotary clubs?

Another example of where young people are going is into the local 20-30 club.

20-30 clubs are made up of young men and women who have a passion for improving the lives of children in their communities. These young leaders serve local kids through hands-on work and fundraising. According to the Active 20-30 International organization it began by realizing a need that wasn't being served by existing service organizations. Is that true? Is not Rotary doing the exact same thing? This probably means that many of the young people have a desire to work with other 20-30 year olds.

This is why so many of the Rotary New Generation clubs are growing in many districts. But what is a New Generations Rotary Club? Let the *Rotary Zone 33 & 34 Membership Blog* help us. It says that New Generation Clubs aren't defined by Rotary, so, in some respects, the New Generation Club is what the Rotarians in that club want it to be.

The main differences are an orientation toward younger Rotarians and a willingness to try non-traditional methods to attract and keep those younger members.

A New Generation Club's focus on younger Rotarians seeks those not just younger in age, but those who are "younger" in their career, in their financial development, in their activity level, or perhaps in their attitude. Non-traditional aspects of a New Generation Club can include meeting times, generally late afternoon or early evening "Cocktail clubs", meeting days, Fridays or weekends, meeting credits for service and   fellowship opportunities, meeting locations (low cost, limited meal or cocktail options), low cost of membership, and stressing smaller hands-on service projects instead of check-writing.

It's as if they have their head in the sand. One club
said, "We're all right, thank you, we have enough
members and we don't need to recruit." It is like a
frog. If you place the frog in very cold water and he's
a bit uncomfortable, he is very active. If you warm up
the water, he goes to sleep. If you continue to heat up
the water, he dies and he didn't even see it coming!
Is that happening in some clubs, and is that what may
happen to clubs who take no membership action.
Does this represent your club?

Have you ever thought about your club being a sleeping frog?

We may not completely understand why some clubs
are not adding members. Putnam in *Bowling Alone*,
states that there is "not a general decline in civic engagement, but merely a reorientation from the 'old
fashioned' to 'contemporary' affiliations, away from
Rotary and the League of Women Voters to Green-
peace and the Sierra Club." He might have said
members are moving to Metro EDGE or 20-30 clubs.

Rotary clubs keep talking about going out and re-cruiting young people into their ranks. We have heard that young people have been raised with a global awareness of everything from political issues to poverty and the environment. We know they have been expected to volunteer by their parents and their teachers and service learning has been on their plate since junior high school.

We have not mentioned change even though we are certainly suggesting that these young people are changing their volunteer directions to groups like Metro EDGE and 20-30 clubs.

What Do We Mean By Change?

Change, by definition, causes at least some degree of frustration. But most change does not occur overnight, it requires a certain amount of work, time and maybe frustration. Sometimes our dilemma is that we want to change and keep everything the way it is.

We like our club the way it has always been, but we feel we must change something if we are to going to bring in those new younger members.

Sydney J. Harris says it much better than I can. "What we really want is for things to remain the same, but get better." Is that a perfect view of your Rotary club? We want to bring in all those younger members, but we really don't want to change anything about the club. Maybe we feel these young folks should just accept things the way they are.

As you visit Rotary clubs it becomes apparent that the club members are aging and while that by itself is not a main issue, since all of us are aging. The real issue is that we have not figured out how to attract younger members into our ranks. Corporate America finds that dealing with age diversity means understanding and relating effectively with people who are different than you. For the first time, a few Rotary clubs have four distinct generations working side by side.

These four generations differ on a number of major issues including how they approach service, work/life balance, loyalty, and authority. It is time to begin to explore exactly what these differences mean and how we can begin to bridge these generations in your Rotary club.

Your reaction to a declining membership might be that you will send out an e-mail blast and expect new members to flock in the door.

Or you take the issue to the board and expect the membership committee to get busy and round up those new members. To tell you the truth, while both of those solutions might help, neither will solve the overall problem. It is time for the organization to take a look at the overall issue of declining membership.

It is not a matter of pushing harder or getting members to accept responsibility for recruiting. It will require some change in the way we plan to attract members and believe me, that is not easy.

Change is difficult for everyone and is particularly difficult for Rotary clubs. Bringing in younger members is going to involve change in a number of areas. Age diversity is a unique feature of club membership and for some reason, more difficult than facing either gender or ethnic diversity.

Increasing the number of young people in a Rotary club will require a change in the methods used for attracting members. It's not a matter of going out and inviting prospects. It is a matter of learning how to attract them. Today's potential member will need to find us through our attraction techniques.

Once attracted they will then start shopping for the one Rotary club that fits their interest and needs. In the words of Bob Dylan, "The Times They Are A-Changin'."

> Come gather 'round people
> Wherever you roam
> And admit that the waters
> Around you have grown
> And accept it that soon
> You'll be drenched to the bone
> If your time to you
> Is worth savin'
> Then you better start swimmin'
> Or you'll sink like a stone
> For the times they are a-changin'.

I am sure that Bob Dylan was not thinking about attracting new members to Rotary when he wrote this song, but it seems so on target. Past RI President Wilf Wilkinson told us back in 2007 that in order for Rotary to survive, Rotary needs to grow. He stresses that "there can never be a point of equilibrium, where we have as many members leaving as we have coming in; there always need to be more coming in then there are leaving." But if your have followed Rotary for the past decade that is exactly what we have done. We add six and lose six members. We just hold our numbers equal but we are not growing.

Understanding Rotary Generations

We have already said that Rotary is aging and we are aware that we have a generation of young people that we hope to attract to Rotary. But first, we need to understand how we can best accomplish this. We even need to understand what we mean by generations.

A generation is a group of people based on their age that share a chronological place in history and share experiences that go with it. These experiences give them-shared beliefs and behaviors. Older Rotarians have shared Rotary beliefs concerning club traditions and practices. It may be those traditions and practices that create separation from your younger members.

As our more senior Rotarians grow older, we need to attract that next generation into the clubs. The natural audience is either the younger generation or baby boomers. Why not both?

Boomers are that group looking toward retirement and they are strong in numbers, over 78 million in the United States alone. They can expect to live to an average age of 83. That means their life expectancy is about 8 years longer than our current senior members and this life expectancy is likely to increase during our boomers lifetimes.

We may be thinking that all we need to do is recruit more boomers and all our membership problems will go away.

The trouble with that thought is that even these new boomer members are growing older and we will continue to face the same issue of a club full of older members. We also need to be aware that engaging members of different ages is even more critical as younger people enter the workforce. I am going to discuss the two youngest generations, Generation X (born between 1965 and 1980) and millennial (born 1981 to 2001).

This millennial generation is the largest generation to date and represents the critical future of Rotary. But neither the Gen X nor millennial are entering Rotary fast enough to replace our older members who are leaving. Clubs that successfully attract multi-generational members will be the Rotary clubs that succeed in the long term.

It will be the wise club that spends time beginning to understand the differences between generations and there are many differences.

Spending time understanding differences will help to avoid tensions between generations. Your younger members may try to jump in feet first, but may not want to do things the way they've always been done. If your club is being driven by members older than 50 years old, then what can we do to attract those younger ones into Rotary?

It is clear in Rotary that our top leadership is and continues to be past district governors, many of which are over 60 years old. And unlike the corporate world, thank goodness, they are not planning to retire and move on. Industry has always retired its senior officers and as the younger managers moved upstairs, change slowly occurred. Rotary is having a difficult time moving those younger members upstairs into leadership roles.

It is interesting to watch the top levels of Rotary International change by bringing in younger professionals in membership and foundation ranks. They go to universities around the world to recruit these younger professionals. The district and club levels of Rotary are not tending to move in the same direction. I realize that those Rotary International professionals are paid staff and the district and club personnel are all members volunteering.

One issue is that most districts are still placing their leadership in the hands of its most senior members and are not engaging those younger members. Those district governors are mostly retired from work and have more time for Rotary, but they may not be keeping up with the changes in public image, communication and social media.

There are a number of clubs working to attract younger members, but it is still only a small minority of clubs and leaders.

It's clear that younger members should be the next wave of Rotary membership.

Netanya Stutz, senior marketing manager of the Washington, D.C.-based American Hotel & Lodging Association tells us that it's important for us to understand what the younger person's needs are and what they want out of a professional organization. She says, "Associations need to start thinking about a succession strategy if they want to still be around in the future."

Our younger members want to make a difference in the world, be heard, and feel like they are contributing. We know they live in a fast world, moving at a fast pace and they wonder why everyone is not moving like they are. While our senior members talk about their latest cruise, these younger members are talking career and family issues. There is a disconnect between generations and it should not be occurring in the Rotary club.

Part of this disconnect is easy to solve. You did it when you changed from a print newsletter to a digital one. You are doing it by changing from a social hour at the local pub to a family-night activity at the local pizza house. You do it by changing from projects relating to the local senior center to working at a crisis center for moms. Don't get me wrong, all the projects taken on by your Rotary club are important, but you need to think about a variety of age-related projects.

The biggest difference between younger members and more mature members is what they expect to derive from their membership.

Younger members demand more of a return on their investment and are less likely to join an organization where they pay a fee without any tangible return or real participation

Generation X expert Rebecca Ryan captures the Xers skeptical attitude in *Sticking Points* by Haydn Shaw. She sees Gen Xers as " a generation of Americans who don't talk to strangers and have little faith in institutions. In other words, Gen Xers are skeptical. They have a difficult time trusting others, they are obsessively self-reliant, and they don't see themselves as joiners of traditional organizations."

Gen Xers are skeptical of all organizations, including Rotary. They will attend meetings only if they find them relevant, but they aren't as interested in membership and don't join committees as enthusiastically as Boomers did. It is abundantly clear that young people don't join just to be members. "They don't discharge social capital responsibility by writing a check and being a member of something. That's characteristic of a past generation." according to Arthur Brooks, PhD, director of the Nonprofit Studies Program at the Maxwell School of Citizenship and Public Affairs at Syracuse University.

Paul Kiser in his blog on Rotary tells us that "Rotary was truly a young professionals networking club at its inception; however, today's Rotary club is a foreign environment to most business people under 45." He tells us "Interestingly, in discussions with Rotarians, I have found we often have no clue as to how young professionals perceive Rotary, and in fact, I have found that some Rotarians have a bias against youth." This is not a good thought, and we all hope that this is not true.

But Paul found that in one case a very prominent local Rotarian was advising clubs to ignore anyone under 40 as a potential member. His reasoning was that, "They have kids and they're not in a place in their career to be a good Rotarian." Paul says, "That was a great attitude...for keeping Rotary an old person's organization."

Younger Rotarians turnover might be high for a number of reasons. They move fast and want to be challenged.

In *Rotary Voices*, David Postic, a member of the Rotaract Club of Norman, Oklahoma tells us how to fix the problem. *"First, wake up. If your meetings or service projects are not more exciting than going to the mall, watching the latest episode of American Idol, or even spending an hour on Facebook, young people will not be engaged and they will not join. Get out into the community and serve. Develop innovative projects that truly make a difference."*

"Second, let go of your club. Give up control. People my age want to feel like they are making an impact. Give young members responsibilities. Listen to their ideas. Most importantly, make them the leaders and let them change things. If you make it a habit to continuously evolve as a club, you will continue to engage young people and flourish. And when clubs flourish, Rotary flourishes. It is as simple as that."

If they become bored with a club, they're gone. Millennial tend to be loyal to people more than organizations.

It is important to get them connected in a hurry when they join a club in order to keep them around.

The younger generations in Rotary are the Millennial, young professionals between 18 and 30 years old and Generation X is roughly between 31 and 45 years old. Both of these generations are the young members Rotary is looking to add to its membership roster.

Millennial are the first generation carried around in huge SUVs with "baby on board" signs in the back window. These are the children of the large "Baby Boomer generation." They are the first group who received a trophy whether they were a winner or not because every child deserved a trophy or you might damage their self-esteem. Sometimes referred to as Generation Y, this group prefers to be called the millennial generation. They are larger than the boomer generation; in fact, they make up nearly a third of the U.S. population. This is the largest generation of young people since the 1960s.

They are unlike any other generation and they grew up during the "digital age" and we saw the impact this generation made during the last presidential election with social media. They were active and showed support for Barack Obama.

They seem to text more than they talk. They text rather than e-mail. They are connected to dozens of social networks and communicate with people all over the globe. They have never been without computers or smart phones. They're well educated, skilled in technology and very self-confident.

To Gen X and Y, formal networks like Rotary may seem time-consuming, not very productive, and limited in structure, in other words they might seem like they are their parent's clubs. They just don't seem to fit their lifestyles. Lisa Johnson in *Mind Your Xs and Ys* tells us, "They can lack immediacy, fun, and a true sense of impact." In many ways it might mean that they are not waiting to fit in but want to find an organization where they fit better.

They are the connected generation that checks Google's websites before applying for college, employment and again, before joining Rotary.

They will likely shop for a Rotary club before joining, and will make their decision based on what they see on their iPhone screen. If the club does not have a current and active Facebook page and a Twitter account sending Tweets regularly, they will likely never show up to see a Rotary meeting. When they do show up they will bring a new style and a new perspective to Rotary. And unless Rotary clubs are willing to adapt, they will find them going out the door almost as fast as they enter.

This generation has not been in the Rotary world for very long, but they are already challenging the status quo.

For one thing this generation is going to show up and expect to have a voice. As Lynne Lancaster in her book, *the M-factor* tells us " Millennial are pushing for new forms of leadership and decision-making based on collaboration." They have skills already developed for cooperation, but we wonder how the older Rotarians will accept this new way of relating.

The Millennial will certainly challenge the ways many of us older Rotarians run our clubs. For example, Boomers will often do what the Millennial call the "death march" where each person reports on his or her work while everyone listens, or pretends to listen. Millennial wonder why these reports can't be shortened and e-mailed to all of us. Millennial are always asking, "How do we get those older members to listen to us? They don't seem to take us seriously."

Millennial are a highly educated group, three quarters are educated beyond high school and over 25% hold college degrees. Another 25% are currently attending college. They are the most racially and ethnically diverse generation ever in America. Millennial are very concerned about social and environmental issues and are very active in community service. Now let's look at those older young professionals, Gen Xers.

Generation X grew up in a very different world than previous generations. Divorce and working moms created "latchkey" kids out of many of these young people. This led to traits of independence, resilience and adaptability.

Generation X feels strongly that they don't want to be micro-managed.

At the same time, this generation expects immediate and ongoing feedback, and is equally comfortable giving feedback to others including those on your Rotary board. They work well in multicultural settings, desire fun in the club and expect to be involved in all club decisions.

Generation X saw their parents get laid off or face job insecurity. Many of them also entered the workforce when the economy was in a downturn. Because of these factors, they've redefined loyalty. This will be reflected in their Rotary career. For example, a Baby Boomer may talk about his dissatisfaction with the club, but figures it's just a part of Rotary. A Gen Xer doesn't waste time complaining, she starts shopping for another club, first online and then by visiting the clubs.

Gen Xers may also challenge clubs to rethink their structure as Gen X members may not have as much time to commit to Rotary as older retired members. Rather than your viewing this as a lack of commitment or interest, this may be an opportunity to think of new ways to engage the younger member. Soon to be over mid 40s, they are resourceful and hardworking.

They are made for Rotary International because they are global and digital.

They work well in multicultural settings. Tamara Erickson in her book *What's Next Gen X?* tells us "Xers became the first generation of youth to develop a global perspective and empathy, often through the televised events that raised funds for and awareness about AIDS, apartheid, world famine and a host of other global issues."

Why is Change So Difficult for Clubs?

If what may be needed in Rotary is change, then maybe we should explore why it is so hard to create. We all have reasons to fear change. It's annoying, overwhelming, frustrating, and time-consuming. But for many Rotarians their club is just perfect the way it is.

They have invested years learning the Rotary way and then all of a sudden everyone is suggesting that we change so many things.

It is the idea of change that is creating most of the stress in Rotary clubs, as the traditions are being challenged and many of the good old ways of doing things are threatened.

In the February 2004 issue of *The Rotarian*, Rester Samse, a member of RI's Membership Development and Retention Committee said…" It helps us really, truly be a part of the family of Rotary by acknowledging that when so many different people come together, so many things happen."

We can certainly agree that bringing women and ethic diversity into our clubs has given us a whole new club environment. If this is true, then why is it so difficult to bring younger generations into the club?

The blog, America's *Best Business Practices*, helps us understand generational diversity when they said,

"It is often difficult for people of different ages to understand each other."

A member of the Rotary Club of Vancouver Chinatown, BC, Canada gives us an interesting view about the need to bring in younger members,

"If a club wakes up one morning and discovers they're old, it can almost be too late."

Many clubs overlook the fact that the majority of their members will be retiring in the next decade and that the generations to follow are radically different from the generations of the past.

But many Rotarians worry that this younger generation, rather than gaining the experience at running their fundraising event, will want to lead it and dismiss the older members suggestions. The senior Rotarians may feel that younger members have completely different values, interests, and needs from the generations before them. This might just be accurate.

According to Sarah Sladek, in her book, *The New Recruit* tells us "everything about this younger generation is new and different, from their values and expectations to the way they communicate and spend their time." She suggests that, "What worked in the past for associations won't work for the younger generations." Rotary is one those associations.

Rotary remains almost entirely governed and supported by the mature and boomer generation, and very few clubs are developing plans and strategies to bring in younger members.

Many of the younger generations refer to today's Rotary as outdated and irrelevant. This might be because they don't feel that Rotary clubs provide anything meaningful or relevant to them. It appears that the younger generation has a distrust of institutions and that has prompted them to value self-reliance and to develop strong survival kills. These skills can be of value to a club only if they value the younger member. Clubs must begin to begin to talk with younger members and begin to understand the differences between generations. Then they must learn to appreciate these unique differences.

After this appreciation comes accommodating these differences to maximize the strengths of each generation. Not easy you say? You are so correct, but let's get started.

First, Gen Xers, our 30 and 40-year-old members are the smallest generation. They are also the most misunderstood and the most skeptical generation. But they are picking up the leadership in most American corporations and this is the leadership that Rotary needs during its next twenty years. These are the club presidents for the coming years of Rotary.

Then, the youngest group, Millennial, are the least understood generation. None of the other three generations understand them.

These millennial, with their revolution in technology, they will be the most productive generation in history which is exactly why Rotary needs to start attracting them into membership.

They are still quite young, but they have the volunteer service drive that is also why we need them to join with us in Rotary.

What Kinds of Change do you need to attract these younger generations?

Change #1 is our club meeting. Maybe it's time to consider changing the old-school meeting format. Maybe it means getting rid of the straight lecture or PowerPoint presentations in order to satisfy an emerging generation of members.

If you motivate the younger member with an inspiring and fun meeting, they will stay. Both Gen Xers and Millennial hate long and boring meetings. Both generations will expect to text and use their laptops to communicate during your meeting. It is not disrespectful; it is their way of keeping connected. Ask them a question during your meeting and they will tell you exactly what is been discussed.

They will question why you sing at the start of the meeting and why are those songs from grandpa's day? And they will question starting the meeting with a prayer. Whose religion are we focusing on? They will suggest a thought for the day, which fits all beliefs.

Change # 2 is communication styles. Think about your website or digital newsletter. Our young people have grown up with Apple, Amazon and Google and expect communication to anticipate their needs and speak directly to them. It may be why they continue to text and study their smart phones during a meeting.

Communication technologies have changed the way we work, play and live, and they will continue to change.

The Web 2.0 networked technology is a defining experience in their lives. If Rotary is going to succeed with this younger audience, you're going to have to get familiar with the communication tools they can't live without.

Remember the younger generation finds their love relationships on e-Harmony and they buy their children's toys on e-Bay, while checking their vacation dreams on Cheaptickets.com. Their Kindle Nook goes with them everywhere and it has over 50 books in digital form. At home their entire movie selection comes right off their Apple TV app.

Art Butler, president of the Plymouth Noon Rotary Club tells a pretty good story in the *Observer & Eccentric*, which demonstrates some of the challenges facing Rotary clubs with aging membership and a need to get younger to survive.

Butler said he knew of one club that fined its members if their cell phones went off during a meeting. Such a rule, Butler contends, could keep younger people, who are connected like no previous generation to technology, out of the ranks of the club.

David Parsons of Springfield Illinois, District Governor of District 6469, says, "Attracting the younger generation is going to mean two things — getting longtime members to embrace new ways of doing things and refocusing the traditional approach."

"Today's up-and-coming generation," he says, "is interested in service, not just sitting at a meal and chit-chatting socially. They want to be actually doing something, getting involved." These younger members have seen the economy go into a recession and watched the dot-com bubble burst. They realize that their employers are less likely to pay for their Rotary membership dues.

They are working hard to support their family and work-related expenses and are aware that Rotary adds to this cost. They realize that they cannot attend every week and are concerned how this will set with the older club members.

Even if Rotary International tells them that they are only required to show up 50% of the time, they sense that the older members do not agree with this.

These younger members are interested in the weekly program and learning, more than the opportunity to gain fellowship. For the young member, the term fellowship has an old ring to it and it appears to them to mean something that the older members need.

For fellowship to attract the younger member it must indicate business networking that they will personally benefit from. They will ask what the return on the investment of their time is going to be. One of their strongest characteristics is the network of friends they have maintained.

This is an area that a Rotary club can push and give value to the young member. It is also why we must bring in a number of young people at the same time.

It is the networking with peers that the young member will treasure and they see value in connecting.

Social media can produce that bridge between generations as both generations are well into it. Even the Boomers like Facebook. According to a recent study, the fastest growing demographic on Facebook is people aged 55+. And many clubs are using Facebook to promote all of their service and fundraising projects.

Art Dearoff from the Rotary Club of Lincoln, California posts almost daily references to Rotary on his club's Facebook page.

Connie Reece, co-founder of Social Media Club International and a boomer herself, says in her presentation "Email Is for Old People" that clubs need to reach out to boomers on social networks, and integrate this outreach with their email marketing strategy. "Your outreach should not be limited to social networks created especially for Boomers." Reece says. But she does say that this boomer group is increasingly on Facebook and Twitter.

Hadley Schmoyer in the newsletter *The Center for Association Leadership* said that a common reason for young people to disengage from groups is that they are not valued. She tells us that we should "let your younger members lead or co-lead projects that affect them. This allows for mentoring and intergenerational connecting."

Thinking that younger members can bring positive changes may open new avenues for your club and be able to bring a new network of young professionals that will be the future in carrying on your mission.

Hadley Schmoyer is a founding board member of *Spark the Wave* and curator for the Portland Harbor Museum, South Portland, Maine. She has a straightforward approach to the attracting of young members. She says, "One thing that most young people have is endless energy, which they are looking to throw into a cause that they care.

This speaks to insuring that the club allows the younger members to suggest projects that the younger members can work with as a group. You will find that incorporating younger members into your Rotary club will add a needed shot of energy and create new directions that can energize the entire club. Hadley says, "If you expect the best from a young member, you will get it."

10 Issues With the Younger Members

There are ten issues confronting younger members
when they consider joining Rotary. The first three
are time, money and family. These three issues will
come up regularly during recruiting talks with
younger potential members. They will ask questions
relating to how much time is expected of members,
how much money does Rotary expect, and how can
my family be involved in Rotary activities.

Issue # 1 is Time.

This might be impacted by the age of the potential
young member and their place in the work world.
They feel that their time is impacted by both work
and family responsibilities. For example, if the Rotarian is older and already retired, then the time concerns are not as critical. But if the young member is
working longer hours or even working at more than
one job, it will be a major concern. If the member has
small children needing care and transportation, then
time again becomes a major concern.

As younger women move into Rotary, childcare usually takes a major role in the time arena.

If both mom and dad are working, then childcare becomes an even stronger issue. It appears that time and the apparent lack of it in today's busy world of work and pleasure is a major issue. With the growth of single moms and single dads, childcare issues become even stronger.

Even with the younger millennial generation time is critical between their dating and social life and the need to focus on their education goals. Education requires money and time and Rotary has needs in both areas as well.

Time becomes a stronger issue because the club requires a weekly meeting for continuing membership in the club. There are options that clubs might consider in relationship to the time concerns. They might hold meetings less frequently than weekly or simply overlook weekly attendance requirements.

Rotary has changed its meeting requirements to only 50% attendance. The 2013 Council on Legislation approved a measure allowing participation in club projects to count toward club attendance requirements. The measure amends the Standard Rotary Club Constitution to provide that a member must attend or make up at least 50 percent of club regular meetings or engage in club projects for at least 12 hours in each half of the year, or a combination of both.

This might make it easier for our younger members to attend service projects or evening events to keep their membership current.

Rotary has also launched a large number of e-clubs that allow members to meet on their home or office computers, either by joining an e-Rotary Club that meets only through electronic media or as a way to make up when you miss your weekly Rotary club meeting. E-clubs meet electronically, conduct service projects, and sometimes also hold in-person meetings.

The Rotary District 7820 website *Time for Rotary.com gives* you a sample of the thoughts prospective members might express about Rotary membership and time.

"With all the things going on in my life, I don't have enough time in the day for Rotary."

"When my life settles down a bit, I'll consider Rotary."

"I would like to give back to my community but what kind of time commitment is involved if I join?"

Issue # 2 is Money.

This is another issue for many, even without considering the current economy. Rotary has always been considered a rich person's game, even if that was a false perception. But still it does require funding for annual dues, weekly meals, and foundation donations.

There is pressure in some clubs to pay fines and to contribute a sustaining fee of $100 to the Rotary Foundation. While this is optional, it might still increase the pressure for those with limited incomes. There are options for clubs to cut the expense of meals by substituting less expensive meals or offering an option to not have a meal. Some clubs allow a member to only pay a small amount for coffee or a soft drink. Others offer a smaller meal at a lower cost to the member.

Even early morning meetings at Starbucks might be an alternative to the more expensive charges.

A few clubs might give up the meals all together and go to a happy-hour format where purchasing anything is optional.

It is a matter of the club trying to fit in to the members' lifestyles.

Rotary District 5170 in their Membership Minute illustrated this point by suggesting two possible solutions to help younger members. They suggest that a club might consider lowering the total cost of membership in your club or they might consider waiving certain fees or expenses for the first year or two.

These young members have invested time and dollars in education and this means most of them carry a heavy student loan package. They graduated from college just when the economy was slow and college placement directors said it was the worse job market for college graduates since World War II.

Many younger professionals say Rotary is simply too expensive. They mean the dues, the cost of meals, travel, meetings, service projects and fundraising. But, it might be that the meals are the most expensive portion of expense that the young member faces. How does a club help the young member to handle those costs associated with Rotary?

PDG Judi Beard Strubing in a fun blog called *blue avocado* gave an excellent response to the issue of the cost of Rotary membership. "Some clubs have smaller initiation fees and lower dues than others. It often depends on whether the club prefers to write checks or do fund-raising, or is more interested in hands-on projects. Meal costs can vary depending on time of day and venue. I've noticed that the costs for lunches in metropolitan areas tend to be higher than in the smaller communities. Some clubs have arranged for a coffee only option for those who prefer not to have a meal. Some of the newer clubs have adopted the "After Five" model, which usually means having a beverage at the meeting (food is optional) and going home to have dinner with the family. And --- Rotary clubs across North America have been assessing, and reducing where possible, costs in light of the tight economy."

Some older members will simply say Rotary has always been a rich man's club. I know they are teasing, but there may be a little truth in the fact that people did not join Rotary until they were in their place in life where they could afford it.

"If you're fifty years old and vice president of a company, you can join a chamber of commerce. If you're twenty or thirty years old, you're not likely to join the chamber or attend $200 dinners to be social or a $25 breakfast. It's not something our age group is going to do," stated F. Anne Harrel, founder of the Boston Young Professionals Association. She is talking about joining a chamber but I think it would apply to a Rotary club as well.

A few Rotary districts have suggested that clubs consider lowering the total cost of membership. They remind their clubs that some younger members are having trouble meeting the financial obligations of club membership. To combat this problem, some clubs have lowered their fees or have a meal only once or twice a month instead of every week. They also recommend that clubs consider waiving certain fees or expenses for the first year or two.

Younger members who aren't yet fully invested in Rotary may be more apprehensive about committing to all of the financial obligations of club membership.

The Duluth Superior Eco club tells us that they have a late afternoon meeting time and an affordable dues structure. For example, their only meal charges are $5 per week for non-alcoholic beverages and snacks.

Once they become involved in your club and dedicated to Rotary's mission, they may be more willing and able to pay the full amount. Many clubs will panic at the thought of lowering dues and fees because it can have a negative budget implication. But these clubs may need to be willing to take a budget loss on the dues to engage and grow a young professional with the club. It might be that a long-term benefit out-weights the short-term risk.

Issue #3 is Family.

These club activities will require a majority of time and money for many younger members. Since the family requires so much more in the way of classes and sports activities these days, it is a problem for many prospective members. Rotary clubs need to be aware that their members want to volunteer with their families and kids.

Young members want their children to get involved and get their hands dirty volunteering with mom and dad. But it takes the club planning ahead and taking on service projects that allow family involvement. Young people want to build houses and playgrounds. They love the concept of Habitat for Humanity and the Rotary House for families with children in a hos-pital.

It may be that the concept of family clubs with both husbands and wives joining the same club along with childcare might become a viable option.

Tom Cross from the Davis (CA) Sunrise Rotary gives a few very insightful comments concerning today's Rotarian and the idea of family.

"I see Rotary & Family as just the tip of the iceberg. The family dynamic has and is changing from when Rotary started. My impression of early Rotarian's Family was made up of one single income and a spouse at home taking care of the family, cooking, and supporting the Rotarian. This allowed the Rotarian to devote 100% of the community service piece of the pie."

It appears that future Rotarians will have to balance family, money, time, and Rotary with all the requirements of both partners working and work/life balance issues.

Henry Bradley III, Past President of the Islandia-Central Islip Rotary Club in Suffolk County, Long Island, New York, states it clearly when he says, "Our club always includes our local youths and young adults in our projects like Food Drives, Towel Drives, etc. Our clubs have several fellowship activities per year that includes family and friends of Rotarians." He feels the key to continue active membership is to open a line of communication between our club and our members' family.

Phillip Jeffries from Rotary District 7260, writes, "I firmly believe Rotary does not pay enough attention to the role that family members can play in promoting membership of Rotary. Perhaps the time has come to look at official family membership, an all-inclusive approach to Rotary, and not just a place where Dad or Mom go to serve."

Issue #4 Balance Between Life, Work and Rotary

The younger members put their emphasis on life before work, which is why boomers used to think of them as "slackers." The truth is that Boomers haven't called them "slackers" for a number of years, but I've heard Gen X managers call Millennial "slackers" and I bet they do not even know where they got the word.

Boomers were the workaholics of the workplace, and then the generation that followed them had been tagged the Slacker Generation.

Many younger members want their life to have less pressure and be a lot more fun. They may be cynical of the corporate world, and be much more family oriented. They are family oriented, maybe because they were the first generation that grew up with divorced parents, two working parents and the experience of being latchkey kids.

They are referred to as the "Family-First" Generation" by *USA Today*. You will see this at Rotary meetings as they bring their children to meetings. It's not because they cannot afford a sitter. It is because they want to share their children with fellow Rotarians.

Men are as likely to be in charge of the households as the boomer wives were. It is a role reversal, which is enjoyed by younger members. They feel that both family members should have the opportunity to raise the children and earn a living.

When you attract younger members into Rotary, it is critical that the club focus on a wide variety of family activities.

These are the activities that interest those younger members that are raising families and they are very focused on family life. Where the boomers, at that same family life stage would ask their parents to baby sit so they could go to a Rotary event, the younger generations will bring the kids along.

It is important to stress to new members that the club wants to involve their family in its activities. But do not promise something that the club is unwilling or unable to do. This is a great discussion topic for an upcoming board retreat or club assembly.

Issue # 5 Diversity

Race, gender and sexual orientation have turned from rigid identity categories to flexible markers in the Rotary world. The younger members are the first generation to become "color blind." Their friends are from any race and ethnic background.

They do not view color, race or sexual orientation as an issue. They are concerned by their older Rotary members inability at times to eliminate prejudice in their conversation.

They expect to see all Rotary clubs contain people of color and women in numbers that mirror the community.

They also expect Rotary to be open to sexual orientation as well. That may be what lead the Rotary 2010
Council On Legislation to adopt   Enactment 10-40
which states that, "No club, regardless of the date of
its admission to membership in RI, may by provi-
sions in its constitution or otherwise, limit admission
in the club on the basis of gender, race, creed, national origin or sexual orientation."

It should be no surprise that Millennial are the most
ethnically and racially diverse generation in American history. According to *The Millennial Legacy*, "58
percent of Millennial are reportedly white or Cauca-
sian and 42 percent were a minority. And it is esti-
mated that because of ongoing immigration, by the
year 2020 these numbers in America will be 56 white
to 44 percent minority." In fact, a January, 2010 *Pew
Research Center Study* revealed that 67 percent of 18-
to-29-year-olds agreed that increasing ethnic and ra-
cial diversity is a good thing. Rotary's Guiding Principles states this desire to continue building
diversity. In its Principles is this statement.

"A club that reflects its community with regard to professional and business classification, gender, age, religion, and ethnicity is a club with the key to its future."

Rotary District 6060 in Eastern Missouri says that "In order to recruit younger professionals, women and others into our clubs, we must also be willing to adapt our activities and traditions to the needs and preferences of our changing membership."

The University of Oregon has the best explanation of how to do this when it said, "Understanding each other and moving beyond simple tolerance to embracing and celebrating the rich dimensions of diversity contained within each individual."

This gives the Object of Rotary value as each club works toward tolerance, respect and a better understanding of all peoples of the world.

Diversity also indicates the respect between the different generations. From the standpoint of the more mature members of Rotary it is positive that the *Pew Research* tells us that millennial "respect their elders and a majority say that the older generation is superior to the younger generation when it comes to moral values and work ethic." This thought will certainly help to cement that relationship between the mature Rotarians and the incoming millennial population.

Issue #6 Volunteering

Many younger Millennial and Gen Xers are already engaged in their communities, in a way their parents never were. They are volunteering, raising money, and working to fight poverty, pollution, disease, and the big issues confronting the world today. Volunteering, on the part of young people, has hit an all-time high.

The *Higher Education Research Institute* reported that some 83 percent of incoming college freshman have volunteered and over 70 percent did it on a weekly basis. The same survey found that two-thirds of college freshmen think it is very important to help other people; and about the same percentage say it is very likely they would do community service during their college years.

Morley Winograd in his book, *Millennial Makeover*, stated, "... in many respects they are more like their grandparents and great-grandparents than they are like their own parents."

Both the mature and the millennial generations are also large in comparison with the generations that immediately proceeded their own.

A desire of the younger generation is to fix the problems they see in the world.

They have been very involved in high school and college service learning programs. Many have traveled overseas on church missions or other nonprofit overseas programs. Their desire for improving the world certainly makes this generation a natural connection with Rotary.

What Rotary offers with its Polio-Plus program and dozens of other world-wide humanitarian ventures including clean water, food and health service programs puts it right on the younger members plate.

The most recent survey of volunteer activity across the nation released by the *Corporation for National and Community Service* demonstrates the "spirit of service" which animates America's newest generation, the millennial.

The *NDN blog* tells us "approximately 1.3 million Millennial offered their time without compensation to non-profit organizations, providing over a billion hours of volunteer service to our nation's communities."

This generation is volunteering in record numbers according to the *USA Today*. Morley Winograd and Michael Hais, co-authors of *Millennial Makeover: MySpace, YouTube, and the Future of American Politics say,*

> ***"This civic generation has a willingness to put aside some of their own personal advancement to improve society."***

One of the most noticeable traits of the millennial generation is that they participate in more community service than either of their parents' generations. Having grown up on Twitter and Facebook, today's youth respect their communities and recognize the importance of staying engaged.

The *Huff Post* states that "as the 2008 elections showed, Millennial proved they could walk the walk and flocked to the voting polls, many for the first time." The group saw in president Obama what they see in themselves: hope, opportunity, intelligence and commitment.

Around the country, Millennial are making a difference in their communities through service. By working within their communities, they are able to create safer neighborhoods through after-school and athletic programs that keep kids off the streets. They improve the quality of education by mentoring and tutoring students in subjects that they find difficult.

Community service appears to be a part of their DNA. "It's part of this generation to care about something larger than themselves," says Michael Brown, co-founder and CEO of *City Year*, which places young mentors in urban schools. "It's no longer keeping up with the Joneses. It's helping the Joneses."

These are the future members that Rotary clubs need to grab.

But the question remains, how do we attract this generation?

Issue #7 Connections

Globalization and technology have been shaping change since the dawn of time. But now Millennial connect with their farthest-flung neighbors in real time, regardless of geography, through online communities of interest. Their friends are all over the world via Facebook, MySpace, Twitter, and Skype.

This younger generation grew up in a "sound bite" era.

Twitter, according to Wikipedia, is a social networking and micro-blogging service that enables its users
to send and read other user messages called tweets.
Tweets are text-based posts of up to 140 characters.
This sound bite has become a distinguishing characteristic of the way young people communicate.

You see them multitasking five activities at once.
They use their smart phone to text, surf the web, find
directions, take pictures and video and check with
friends and work. Facebook is on at all times and An-
gry Birds is on their screen 24/7.

They spend time on Craigslist to find what they want
to buy and visit the App store everyday to find something new for their tablets. Younger folks are using
their social networking sites to further their volunteer efforts.

 Ron Alsop in his book *The Trophy Kids Grow Up*, tells
us about a start-up called Project Agage, using the
social network site Facebook to launch the *Causes*
program with the goal of empowering individuals.
Alsop adds that "Facebook users are being encour

aged to recruit their network of friends to support their pet cause." Could this pet cause become a Rotary pet cause?

Of all the talents that younger members bring to the Rotary club, being technologically savvy is their greatest skill contribution. They are constantly connected as they listen to their iPods or send text messages, all while working on a critical project.

Social media is at the heart of their world. This allows them to connect with co-workers and friends around the world at great speed. The electronic capabilities of younger members are extraordinary.

Your club website and Facebook page are the primary locations that younger people go to find out about your club.

If it is out of date or appears boomer-centric, they will pass.

In a Facebook page from Rotary International, which asked questions concerning how younger people might advise Rotary Clubs about attracting new members, one younger Rotarian said, "A major mistake of clubs is not to invest any time in keeping websites up to date and interesting."

This is the first place people will go when they are searching for a club and if there is nothing there or it looks boring, that would be a big minus.

The Rotary Club of Milwaukee is working hard these days to stay technologically relevant 95 years after it was founded. "The view is that service organizations are dead and membership is dying," says Mary McCormick, executive director of the Rotary Club of Milwaukee. "We're constantly holding up the mirror to figure out how to continue to be relevant."

A search of their website shows that they are connected to Facebook, Linkedin, and YouTube as well as offering videos and podcasts. It is important to realize that Rotary International has a presence on Facebook, Twitter and LinkedIn and sponsors discussion groups on those sites.

We all have become attached to our cell phones and you just need to stop into a Starbucks to see that everyone is either on their smart phones or at least it is sitting on the table near them. Today it seems that all generations feel this need for constant connection. But your younger members have grown up with this connection.

They have never known a world without wi-fi or the web. A common thought is that they would feel naked without their cell phone. They will tell you that their best conversations are on Twitter.

Paul Engleman in *The Rotarian* talks about the Rotary Club of Houston and their Facebook and Twitter accounts. Current club president Michelle Bohreer says that about half the club's 240 members are on Facebook. "They are not fully engaged yet, with photos and all, but they are getting there," she says. Bohreer is certain that the club's activity on Facebook is having a positive impact. "People come up to me and say they learned something about Rotary from our Facebook page," she says.

"Younger people are attending our meetings and they say, 'I saw you on Facebook.' We're getting a great response."

According to Ron Alsop in *The Trophy Kids Grow Up* "Millennial aren't just passive voyeurs on the Internet, they are also prolific content creators." This speaks to the need for Rotary leaders to involve them into the process of starting to develop meaningful social media for their clubs.

If your club needs to improve the way it communicates both internally and externally to your community and you realize that social media is part of the answer, your millennial members will be your answer.

Issue #8 Being Green

This generation is not turning green, they are green, very concerned about the environment, and willing to volunteer to save it. Green is no longer a movement, it is an expectation. These young people have lived most of their lives in a green society. They live with less and phrases like carbon footprint and renewable energy are in their everyday vocabulary.

According to a survey by *Cone and Amp Insights*, "nearly 80% of millennial say they prefer to work for a company that cares about making contributions to society." If this generation turns out to the most service driven generation as the literature makes it seem is possible, they will be perfect for Rotary.

"Their desire to do volunteer work, both in their local communities, and even to take on global challenges, makes them a dead ringer for Rotary membership."

U.S. President Barack Obama expressed satisfaction that young people are much more aware and focused about environmental issues than his generation.

This interest in the environment is a natural connection for young people and Rotary. Since 1905, Rotary members worldwide have implemented thousands of environmental projects, from digging wells and creating conservation areas to starting community-recycling programs.   This started to grow during the Rotary year 2008-09 with the birth of a revitalized "green movement" within Rotary.

Even though millennial are known to be the most environmentally educated generation, they often do not take action on their extensive knowledge, which is a strong reason to get connected with this younger generation. Rotary might supply the vehicle for their volunteer green movement.

 A new Rotary club spanning the border between Minnesota and Wisconsin has put a focus on helping the environment while reaching out to younger members. The Rotary Club of Duluth Superior Eco has adopted a decidedly ecological theme in both name and service projects. Each month, the club participates in projects that focus on making a positive impact on the environment or local community. Current projects have included pulling buckthorn at a local nature center, Dragon Boat Festival Recycling and doing a Beach Sweep on the Lester River.

Amy Haney was the 2010-2011 Duluth Superior Eco Club President and she tells us "This Club truly fits my lifestyle as I am a hands-on person who cares about our environment. Our club members have a commitment to hands- on, environmentally friendly service projects. Their website tells us that their club members have a commitment to hands-on, environmentally friendly service projects

Issue #9   Entitlement

Many Rotarians feel that this millennial generation is the entitled generation. According to Michael McQueen in *The New Rules of Engagement*, "this generation exhibits a high self-esteem and confidence fostered by the constant encouragement they have received throughout their lives."

They seem to have the expectation that they will receive exactly what they want. Sometimes it appears that they expect praise before they have earned it and that they ignore the hierarchy.

It may be that they feel that the Rotary leadership simply takes too long to reach a decision about funding a grant or moving a project along. We need to realize that this is a generation that has been raised to expect a lot and to ask for what they want.

Millennial members will want loads of attention and guidance. They will want to know how they're doing on a service project weekly, even daily.

"They were raised with so much affirmation and positive reinforcement that they come into the workplace needy for more," says Subha Barry, managing director and head of global diversity and inclusion at Merrill Lynch & Co. This is an issue that the club leadership needs to face when bringing on these younger members.

Your younger members might tend to be highly opinionated and fearlessly challenge the board and older members. Status and hierarchy don't impress them much.

They want to be treated like colleagues rather than subordinates and expect ready access to all club leadership to share their brilliant ideas.

Clubs may have to bend a bit and adapt to these younger generations. Club leadership may have to show these young members how their work makes a difference and why it's of value to the club. Smart boards will listen to their young members' opinions, and give them some say in decisions.

Issue #10   A Need for Speed

It seems that this generation does not like to wait. They know only one speed-fast and not just in their video games. After all, they search on the web for everything rather than finding a book. They "google" all the information they desire and for most of them the Internet is way too slow. They can text and talk at the same time and will be checking their texts, Facebook messages and be twitting while participating in the Rotary meeting. Every instant message needs to draw an instant response from them.

You have to remember that these folks do not operate at the same speed that you do.

You might wait until the 6 p.m. news comes on to catch up on the events of the day. But the younger ones start when they wake up with their news blast on their smart phones which by the way are sleeping with them in bed.

The *Business Insider* tells us that 90% of 18-29 year olds sleep with their smart phones and half of them will check their phones immediately if they wake up during the night.

This generation is called the Now Generation because
they demand information as it occurs. With the dom-
inance of social media, the millennial expect real-
time reporting so they feel they are in the thick of
things even when they are sitting comfortably at
home.

Twitter and Facebook status are an integral component in the lives of millennial who regularly upload
photographs on Instagram so they may share their
news in real-time with friends and colleagues.

Thanks to being surrounded by technology, your
younger members have a need for speed. Instant
gratification is commonplace in their book; waiting
around is definitely a foreign concept. From sending
emails to nailing a presentation, they expect to see
results pretty quickly. They are driven by immediate
results.

It is no wonder they criticize the average Rotary meeting as being too slow.

They have no patience for your paper or even a digital newsletter and they wonder why you are not connecting with tweets or at least texting the information.

In Thom Rainer's book *The Millennial* the issue of speed was expressed by a millennial this way.

"I believe social media needs to be electronic because anything in a print format is not fast enough to keep pace with my social life."

Getting Them to Join

When it comes to younger members, some Rotary clubs seem perplexed by this unique and dramatically different generation. These young people are not joining organizations in the numbers or with the same enthusiasm and commitment as prior generations.

They are just very selective about how they spend their time and whom they spend it with. Younger people have to feel a sense of trust and belonging before joining a service club.

Young people grew up in front of the television set and their laptop computers. Baby Boomers like to socialize and network, while younger members prefer meeting in small groups and communicating by texting.

Rotary continues to focus on the weekly meeting, which provides a sense of fraternity to Boomers, but does not have the same appeal to younger members. One concern that continues to show its head is that many young people consider Rotary, as an older persons club. That is understandable since club membership does reflect a high number of over 50 year olds. We know that 89% of all Rotarians are over the age of 40.

The *Oakland Press* in Pontiac Michigan stated that younger people are still feeling called to serve but that they are not joining service clubs. They discuss one young professional who lives in one of the near-midtown neighborhoods that have become settling points for the city's growing young professional class. She's a member of a handful of boards for assorted civic and professional organizations. And, like many other young people, she's an active volunteer. But a service club? "I would have no idea how to be involved with clubs like Lions or Kiwanis," she said. She's hardly in the minority.

Service clubs such as Kiwanis, Rotary or Lions all are growing across the world, yet seem to have lost favor with the younger generation as they enter the prime formative years of career life.

She adds "as a high school student, I saw how Rotary-sponsored programs and scholarships worked and had immediate contact with a lot of community leaders. But to be in Rotary, you have to be sponsored."

As an adult, I know no one currently in Rotary, nor have I been approached about joining."

Don Tapscott in his book *grown up digital* tells us that " for the growing numbers of young people trying to achieve social change, there is a sea of change under way, ranging from civic activities to political engagement. He illustrates this by telling us "if you understand this generation, you will understand how our institutions and society need to change today."

Five Key Innovative Attracting Strategies

Innovative attracting strategies can lend Rotary clubs an image of being cool and on the cutting edge. These five strategies will help you to attract your audience of younger prospects. They are 1. Social media, 2. Creating a sense of community, 3. A relevant meeting format, 4. Limiting club expectations, and 5. Being flexible with your expectations.

 Let's explore each of these strategies.

1.The use of social media as a recruiting tool has more credibility with the younger prospects than anything in print media. But social media sites like Facebook must continue being updated to attract this younger audience.

The value of Facebook is expressed by Hulya Aksu in *Critic Mania* where she says that "Many of the college-students who grew up using Facebook during its inception, are now adults in their thirties with kids of their own. And they're connected not only to the younger generation but to older generations as well."

 Facebook has a strong value in communicating the Rotary message to all of the club members, not just the younger ones. It is interesting to note that Seventy-two percent of Facebook users are between 25 and 54, and that Facebook is used primarily by adults of both sexes, but significantly females in the prime of their active professional careers.

Rotary International is quite clear when they stated in *The Rotarian* that

"If the future of Rotary depends on attracting younger members, then the future of Rotary depends on social networking."

Rotary International is living up to their statement as their Facebook page has more than 35,000 fans, its LinkedIn group has more than 7,000 members, and its Twitter account has more than 6,000 followers.

2. Rotary will have to think about providing services and creating a sense of community. One way to accomplish this is by being a resource for members' career development, offering programs and services to help at every stage of their working life through retirement.

We need to remember that this younger generation is changing both jobs and careers on an everyday basis.

Research indicates that the average young employee changes jobs every 1.3 years.

This certainly affects their membership in Rotary as these young members change jobs and locations. That is a challenge to building a sense of community as your members relocate on a continual basis.

The Red Rock Rotary Club near Las Vegas expressed their sense of community by working to clean up a trail at Red Rock Canyon. "It was good to be out there with our group in the fresh air and do something that's pretty easy and that we all enjoy," said Patrick Sullivan, charter president. "It's definitely more fun with a group of people," said Jennifer Weed, member of the Red Rock club. "You get more interaction, and you get more done. Plus, it builds a sense of community."

3. A relevant meeting format is very important since it appears that younger Rotary members are typically less comfortable in social settings than Baby Boomers. They value the Rotary meeting as a learning environment where the take-home value is large.

This could be a result of the dramatic changes in their work lives.

It is certainly more difficult to have the club be relevant to their careers and to their communities if they do not feel the meeting format works for them.

Chuck Underwood, founder of The Generational Imperative tells us "clubs must earn younger members attendance by making the meeting relevant to their careers and their lives."

But the key is that if Rotary does not offer meetings that young people feel are worth the time they spend on them, they will lose them.

With so many time pressures on their personal and professional lives, people will look carefully at Rotary to determine if it is adding to or helping them cope with their time concerns.

4. A big factor in getting younger people to join Rotary is how much time does the club expect the member to give to accomplish the tasks. If members believe a large amount of time is required to attend meetings and projects to get value, they may conclude that membership in not worth their investment. They will be concerned if they feel that by agreeing to serve in a leadership role, they'll spend all their time in meetings and hardly have time for their families.

The other concern that the younger person faces is in convincing their employers that joining Rotary is a good use of their time. Particularly if some of their time will be taken from their workday. In the past this time was considered well spend and that has changed over the past decade or two. Even chambers of commerce are seeing many employers less willing to support the cost of membership.

5. The key will be to show our new members just how flexible we can be with the limited amount of

time that this audience has to give. We also must re-alize that young members will only volunteer if the work is meaningful and if they can have input. You must understand that the young members will have time there for the taking, but only if you approach them in the right way.

They will only share their time with organizations they figure are in synch with their values and that offer them an opportunity to create meaningful experiences.

Meaningful experiences need to follow their green and environmental patterns and this needs you to create a pattern of creative community service. We have been talking about the younger members desire for meaningful community service and making the meetings more focused and in keeping with a solid learning environment. But just how do we attract these younger members?

So, How do we Attract Younger Members?

RI President Bill Boyd said it so correctly when he said "If we don't get enough young people in Rotary, then Rotary will die." A statement that I believe most Rotarians will agree with, but how do we accomplish this task?

If our Rotary International membership base has 89% of its members being over the age of 40 and if many of the older members are going to pass away in the next decade where does that leave us?

"One thing that Rotary has struggled with is attracting younger professionals, getting people interested in this very traditional organization," said Betsy VanDusen, president of the Red Rock Rotary Club near Las Vegas, Nevada. "So they recruited a couple of the more established Rotarians to begin a New Generation club. "I think the first few meetings there were two of the senior Rotarians and then about four or five of us who didn't really know what we were getting into, but we thought we would check it out." Betsy said, "The idea of service and giving back and networking and establishing a community, for me, was really attractive, and I think that's what also drew a lot of other people, too."

 The Red Rotary club now has over 25 members ranging in age from 25 to 50. "Our vision statement is fairly simple and it's community, friendship, and service," VanDusen said. "And that is really what we're trying to accomplish with the group, trying to build community amongst ourselves and giving back to others. It's people having a good time and enjoying ourselves, while expanding our horizons."

"It is very interesting that when Paul Harris started Rotary in 1905, the original four members were in their late thirties and early forties."

Rotary is now putting an increased emphasis in the RI Membership Development Division to better target younger professionals ages, 30-45 old.

A Rotarian Focus Group in Los Angeles in June, 2008 found that the key reasons that they wanted to add younger members into Rotary was:

- They bring the energy/strength of youth.

- They bring a new vision to the club.

- They help to introduce newer technology to the club.

- Their impact increases the number and frequency of club social activities.

- They bring great ideas for club program speakers and expand the club's contacts and network.

- They can bring the club closer to the community because they have more contacts within the community.

- They can be a source of greater ethnic diversity.

- They provide for the "perpetuity of the club."

I think no one can argue with these strong and positive reasons for bringing younger people into our clubs, but the critical item is how to do it. These eight items are certainly things that every club would like to add to their vision statements.

The Newsletter for Rotary District 1170 said it clearly, "Historically, Rotary has always been an elitist organization to which people wanted to belong. In today's busy world that is no longer the case, and potential members in the community need to be identified and nurtured. In most cases today's young people will not beat a path to your door."

Years ago, when you were in a certain business you almost had to belong to a service club to be successful, but it's not that way anymore. Business support has waned. In many companies the difficult economy is eliminating company pay practice to have upper management employees belong to the key service clubs in town.

Past Rotary Director Ron Beaubien said Rotary and
other traditional service organizations, including
Jaycees, Kiwanis, and Lions, are losing members,
even though volunteerism is on the rise among 25- to
54-year-olds. He calls for "progressive" changes that
will give Rotary a more flexible structure. Beaubien
says

"Younger members will not join boring Rotary clubs that just meet and eat,"

Jim Henry, membership coordinator from Rotary
Zone 34 said "Unless I mistake its seriousness, the
membership decline in North American Rotary clubs
needs, no, demands bold persistent experimentation
in order to reverse course. To pursue new and retain
existing members by doing the same thing over and
over again expecting different results is lunacy.
Common sense says to try different approaches. If
the   different approach doesn't work, admit it and
try something else. But above all, try something!"

In the blog titled *Grow Your Business* Russell White

speaks about why Rotary Clubs are losing member-ship. He says "Rotary groups have an attendance re-quirement and a rigid schedule of meetings and this is what is wrong with these groups: the model no longer fits the business world."

White goes on to say, "Today's business world is flu-id, leaders are schedule challenged, and people only want to pay for exactly what they want and attend only those meetings that interest them." He makes his point by telling us we no longer buy a CD for the one song on it we liked. Today people pay by the song, when they want it, 24/7. No more paying for what you don't want to hear and no more waiting on store hours to buy it.

Business gatherings are now the same way." He fur-ther states that, "the younger generation of upcoming leaders are more expense focused, more immediate results oriented and more mobile. They do not iden-tify as closely to their geographic location, traveling freely for business and pleasure and often working for companies hundreds of miles away." He states,

"If Rotary Clubs want to increase in-volvement and attendance of young-er, more active leaders, they need to create better programs and drop membership requirements."

Truly the clubs that fail to engage the younger gener-ations will age noticeably and eventually become ob-solete. Those clubs that are trying to attract younger members need to realize that younger members have completely different values, interests, needs, and wants from the generations before them.

And these younger generations will not respond to the recruiting efforts of the past.

You cannot just add a Facebook page or blog and ex-pect the new younger generations to come running.

Are younger members difficult to attract?

If everything we are saying about those 21-45 year old folks indicates that they are a perfect connection to Rotary, then why are they so hard to attract?

Remember that I said that this generation is skeptical and they do not trust everything the prior generations says. Put yourself in their shoes and go visit the average Rotary club. What do you see when you walk in the door? A group of older men are sitting around the table. And these men are singing some song from the 40's or earlier. They all sit together, and do not invite you to join their table? There are only a handfull of women present and almost no one of color. Maybe there was one person under the age of 40. You are not really surprised since all your friends told you what you would find.

They said it would look like their Dad's club, if not grandpa's club.

They are not surprised, since they did what comes natural to their generation. They checked out the club's website. The first club they thought to visit, did not even have a website. The one that did have a website, the website was way out of date. They checked for the club Facebook page, but could not find one.

Younger members will join Rotary if they see the value and are provided with a sense of belonging, given adequate opportunities to contribute, and if their participation is valued. This is asking a lot of Rotary clubs.

It is asking you to consider making some changes, and change is hard. You have a fun place where you go each week to be with your friends. Friends, who by the way are very similar to you, you brought many of these people into Rotary and they are fine Rotarians.

If your club is going to appeal to this younger generation, they must be able to think in a different way, which in many cases means a complete repositioning of the organization's marketing efforts.

It is interesting that most Rotary clubs are finding it to easier to bring ethnic diversity into the club than age diversity.

The focus group of the Membership Development Division of Rotary found that "It might be easier to bring in ethnic diversity than generational diversity, depending on how great the gap has become between the club's average age and the younger professionals age."

They also stated that a younger professional might be intimidated or turned-off by the formality and ritual associated with many Rotary clubs. The truth, as stated by many of the younger members, is that they are looking for a more comfortable and relaxed environment where they can have fun and still get things done.

It seems to be the ritual that they object to, and they want short meetings that get more to the point and as they say, "accomplish something." They are busy with work and home responsibilities, and they don't want to attend meetings unless the club has a meaningful program.

Remember that a one key reason they join is to continue to expand their learning curve.

There are many reasons given for why younger people don't join Rotary.

But the most critical reason that younger people don't join is that they don't know anything about Rotary."

I know that when I aged out as the President of the Jaycees, which occurred when I was reaching thirty years old. I did not know much about Rotary. I knew that there was a Rotary club in town, but it seemed that this was for those older and much more successful men in town. The truth is that I did not ask and probably more importantly, no one asked me to come visit the Rotary club. It took me many years to discover the value of a Rotary membership. If one of those older professionals in town had invited me to lunch, I might have considered joining Rotary much earlier. I can only guess that they felt their club had enough of the right kind of Rotarians already sitting in those seats.

So why is it that the majority of Rotary members do not actively recruit members? Well, these members attend the weekly Rotary meeting, listen to the Membership Minute, and go back to work after the meeting. But, when they talk to a fellow non-Rotarian, it never occurs to them to talk about their club. They might talk about a Rotary project, but they fail to suggest that their friend join them.

Since they generally do not associate with a younger crowd, it is easy to see why they don't invite any young people to be their guest at their Rotary club. But these same business leaders see young people at their chamber meetings and at their place of faith, but never consider asking them to join them at Rotary. I assume that they do not focus on Rotary membership.

We have to focus on membership in order to be stronger recruiters.

But Recruiting comes after we attract these young people to think about Rotary.

What does focus mean? I think it means being aware of the need in Rotary to bring in fellow professionals. I think of Stephen Covey's classic text, *7 Habits of Highly Effective People* where he discusses the three steps of seeing, doing, and getting. This is so clear to me. You first must see a prospective member. Then you must invite them to be your guest at Rotary. And lastly, you must ask that person to join Rotary.

It seems that attracting new members of any age is easy, but only if we focus on it. The key to attracting anyone to Rotary is figuring out why someone might be interested in Rotary. There are a number of reasons why members join Rotary. The top six includes networking, social, learning, recognition, fun, and service. Let's explore these top six reasons.

First: Networking is the same as building fellowship and that is one strong reason why people join Rotary. The truth is that you only increase business contacts by increasing fellowship. Many members feel that Rotary is not a networking club. They think of networking clubs like BNI or LeTip, or their local chamber. True, networking is not our primary purpose, but it is a major network for many of our members.

It works so well because of the Four Way Test. In other words, we trust each other and have no fear of recommending a member to anyone.

Networking is particularly interesting to our young

members who are still building their contact lists.

Since Rotarians are the movers and shakers in your town, it is certainly a valuable reason why the younger members state this as their primary reason for joining.

Rick Frishman in his book Networking Magic says it so clearly this way.

"Wherever people congregate, networking opportunities exist."

He adds that most good networkers join groups where they can make good contacts and incorporate them into their networks.

Groups like Rotary are ideal for networking because they bring together like-minded people who share common backgrounds, interests and goals. Frishman tells us that service organizations "which include the Masons, Kiwanis, Elks, Lions, and Rotary Clubs provide outstanding venues for networking."

Second: Social means that your club works hard on fellowship activities.

Many people join when they are new to a community and it is a key way to meet fellow professionals in the community.

You will find that you tend to develop and grow strong relationships with fellow Rotarians and their families.

It is interesting to note that this was my prime reason to join Rotary. I had arrived in Elk Grove, California, having moved from Southern California, 400 miles south. I literally knew nobody in the City of Elk Grove or in the region of Sacramento. The first weekend I arrived in town I looked in the *Elk Grove Citizen*, our local newspaper and saw that there was a Wine Tasting/Garage Sale that very evening. It just happened to be a Rotary fundraiser, but the reality is that I like wine and my wife likes garage sales. So we drove on down there and almost before I got inside the event two people started talking to me about Rotary. They invited me to share lunch with them and I did that at their club meeting the following Wednesday at noon. A few weeks later I was inducted as a Rotarian in the Rotary Club of Elk Grove.

I know you are thinking wow! How easy that was. Did I mention seeing, doing, asking? They did see me walking in the door, they did ask me to join them for lunch, and they invited me to become a Rotarian. How easy was that?

It was that the newspaper article that attracted me, but when I showed up they took the time to notice that I looked interested in what they were doing and then they invited me to their club.

Genevieve Flight, now a member of the Rotary Club of London, reported that at her previous club, she was reprimanded after she brought her three-year-old to a meeting. A club officer warned her never to bring her son again.

Family activities are critical to attracting younger members into clubs.

She suggested that Rotary International do more to encourage clubs to welcome Rotarians with children. "This is the best way forward towards getting more younger members into Rotary," she wrote.

Kim Isagor gave us the opposite viewpoint in *The Rotarian.* "Our club had not yet broken the baby barrier. We're a young and jovial group, but I had trouble envisioning an infant blending in at our weekly breakfasts. After a three-month leave, I stuffed a diaper bag with pacifiers, blankets, diapers, wipes, onesies, and enough spit-up rags to mop up the entire restaurant. Scott and I loaded up the car and hoped for the best. It didn't take long to realize that my concerns were unfounded; the welcome from the members of our club – the Rotary Club of San Luis Obispo Daybreak, California, USA – couldn't have been warmer. Soon enough, Wes had a better attendance record than many of the grown-ups. The wait staff started setting out a high chair for us in advance – near an exit, in case we needed to make a speedy departure. Fellow Rotarians joked that Wes was the founding member of a brand-new club they called "Romperact."

"You're bringing them everywhere else. Why aren't you bringing them here?" says Christine Byrne, past president of the Rotary Club of Casco Bay-Sunrise (Portland Area), Maine. Though she acknowledges that some clubs are more child friendly than others, Byrne says people with kids in tow will feel less self-conscious if they remember that they're not the only parents in the room. Byrne's son Jack, 7, has long been a visitor to club meetings. He puts on a nametag and even contributes "happy dollars" when he has something to share. "Kids get it, and they do listen," Byrne says.

Third: Learning is critical to our younger members and many of them join to enhance their resumes and create meaningful learning relationships.

The weekly program is a wonderful source of knowledge to be gained from the outstanding club programs.

This is why it is so important to generate an outstanding roster of speakers for your club. Too often the club speaker is a local nonprofit asking for help. There is nothing wrong with that once in a while, but not a different nonprofit asking your members for help every week. The key to program success is a variety of program topics and outstanding speakers.

When I was club president I used a technique for programs that I have shared around my district.

I decided there are usually four weeks most months, so I would invite a business owner or manager to talk about the state of business in my community the first week. On week two I invited a governmental speaker, such as a city council member, fire chief, police officer, or city employee. This would give the club members an inside view of city government.

On week three, I invited a local nonprofit agency and let them educate the club on what they do to help the community.

The fourth week the speaker came from Rotary. This might have been another club president or a district officer. This gave the club an opportunity to learn more about youth opportunities like RYE or RYLA. It might be a talk on Polio Plus or the Foundation.

We attempted to follow the Rotary monthly themes as best as we could. For example in August we had a membership speaker talk about the Ignite Membership Program. When the month had five weeks, it was time to hold a club assembly.

Fourth: Recognition is critical to every club. Many do not have a strong way of rewarding their hard working members. It is simply a matter of saying thank you and patting your members on their backs.

Rotary needs to be strong about giving recognition for work well done.

It is fun to honor a different club member every week for something special that they have accomplished.

It might be the membership chair or the fundraising event coordinator that just completed raising all that community service money. It might be fun to give an award to the Quiet Rotarian or the outstanding Greeter each month.

Sometimes clubs consider fines as recognition, but I think that misses the point. This is so much more effective when the club knows it is recognition rather than a fine. To your younger members fines tend to sound like grandpa's Rotary club. Many clubs are encouraged to share their triumphs and happy occurrences through happy dollars...School rivalries are fun and also encouraged but fall more under the vicinity of bragging...so touting a favorite collegiate team will be welcome and encouraged, but subject to a "Bragging Happy Dollar." When offering sad news about a collegiate team the Sgt. at Arms will take pity and accept a $1.00 "Sad Dollar."

Fifth: Fun is probably the strongest need for every member young or older. If the club meeting and the service projects are not fun, then members will lose interest. Social activities that involve the whole family need to have fun as a prime attribute of the event.

We all work hard at arranging fundraising and service events; therefore you need to insure that they are fun as well. Why not have a board position that insures that the club has a number of fun events per quarter. Maybe a "fun director."

My club holds a Rotary After Dark event every month and it has the purpose to be both social and fun. We make sure that it is held in a fun location and that we do not make it a Rotary business session. We invite the partners and family members to insure that everyone enjoys the event.

This younger generation expects to find fun in their work, education, and social life.

The Rotary Club of Fremont, Washington, hired a sitter to help at its evening meetings at Hale's Ales. At the start of each meeting, the children lead the Pledge of Allegiance. At the end, they ring the bell. In between, they retreat to watch movies, color, and eat dinner; they also may choose to eat with the adults.

Once a month, the kids help make sandwiches for a local homeless shelter. "It's a meeting for them too," says club member Shoshanna Osterfeld, whose children are four and six. "They get together. They talk about their week. It's a wonderful experience."

Sixth: Service is the number one venture of any Rotary club. We arrange both community and international service activities. It is through the Facebook pictures following a service activity that we get that good feeling about all that hard work we gave. It is always fun to see pictures of our club service in the local newspapers or on television.

True "Service Above Self" projects are the key to Rotary attraction and retention. This is a wonderful opportunity to involve the youth committees and Interact members. My club has a community garden that the three Interact clubs work to plant with organic vegetables. These are sold for a little income for the Interact clubs and those not sold are donated to the local food bank.

How Can We Make Rotary More Inviting?

If you don't like something, change it. If you can't change it, change your attitude.

Maya Angelou

This quote by the well-known author and poet Maya Angelou might have more truth in it than we want to admit. The Bloomberg BusinessWeek Blog wrote that constant change is a business reality, and organizations must continually adapt to their environments to stay competitive or risk becoming obsolete.

As you review these five questions think about your district and club leadership. These five questions may be helpful in determining the likelihood that a major change will succeed or fail:

First: How is the vision different, better and more compelling with this change?

Second: Are the leaders personally committed to this change?

Third: Does the organization have the capacity to make this change?

Fourth: How ingrained is the current culture and is this change harmful or helpful?

Fifth: Will this change actually deliver the identified outcomes?

When asked what our clubs could change to make Rotary more inviting to younger members, here are a few suggestions from a wide variety of clubs.

-Switch to an evening format with only optional beverages and hors d'oeuvres.

-Make sure the meetings are interesting, fun, and to-the-point.

-Ease up on some of the rules for attendance.

-Reduce some of the formality in meetings.

-Lower the cost for meeting meals.

-Induct several young members at once, instead of recruiting them one at a time.

-Conduct service projects that are likely to appeal to younger members consider waiving certain fees or expenses for the first year or two.

Change starts when members are dissatisfied with the current situation.

Many of the younger members stated that they do not want any membership rules or expectations changed for them. They want to be full Rotarians, but that they hope that the clubs will consider making it easier for all Rotarians to meet attendance and monetary requirements in this difficult economy.

Don't be surprised that when you suggest changes intended to help the younger members, a few will object to any changes. It's just human nature I guess.

We are all hearing that unless we generate enough younger members, the clubs will slowly get smaller and smaller. This may be true in the long run but certainly we need to attract all generations into Rotary for the clubs to continue to be strong community service avenues.

 Even if 89% of your members are over 40 does not mean the club will disappear in a few years. In that figure are a number of 40, 50, and 60-year-old members. And these folks are good solid Rotarians and they are not planning to leave.

The real issue may be that we should be looking to attract all ages, gender, and diversity into our clubs.

A stronger concern might be the decreasing size of many of our clubs. I am working as assistant governor with two clubs that are in the eight-member stage. This is a problem. With that small a number you face an issue with the number of individuals willing to be president of the club.

This book is not aimed at retention, but I think it is as big an issue with today's Rotary clubs as the small number of new members being added annually. But let's move forward with the healthy concept of attracting new people into Rotary.

I am not suggesting that bringing younger members to your club is magic that is missing. It is wonderful to attract those younger members and their excitement will be great for both them and the club. But we know that inviting anyone to Rotary is offering him or her an opportunity that cannot be paid for with any amount of money.

We need to discuss why anyone would illustrate a lack of interest in joining such a strong organization as Rotary. But are their unique reasons that the younger person, male or female might use to say no to joining Rotary? Are there secrets to membership?

Membership Secrets...Are There Any?

Many members attend membership seminars to try and find the secrets to membership recruiting.

There truly are no secrets to recruiting, but there is the opportunity to apply a few very simple techniques.

For example, when you attend any community function, you have an opportunity to market your Rotary passion. As you meet new community members, you need to learn about their experiences, personality, and priorities so that you don't waste time talking about something that doesn't appeal to them.

Your words alone will not convince people to join Rotary. The more time you spend talking, the less time you will spend listening. The faster you talk, the more desperate you will sound. Give just enough information about Rotary to help excite the prospect to attend lunch or breakfast with you.

After your first contact, present an invitation to meet over a cup of coffee to discuss their interest in Rotary. This first meeting is the time to connect with your prospect and for them to connect with you. The fastest way to connect is to show a genuine interest in your prospect's life. Ask about their family and friends. Find the prospect's passion and interests. Ask about their career and educational background. See what other nonprofit or volunteer experiences they have.

Try to find out if they have the time to conduct service projects. Insure that you tell them the true cost of Rotary membership in dollars. It was always easy for me to avoid the truthful answer to exactly how much Rotary costs. I would tell them the weekly charges for the meal and even the annual dues but would overlook the Rotary Foundation, sustaining membership fees and other special dinners and events. I think most clubs tell their potential members that Rotary will cost between $1000 and $2500 a year. You do not do this to scare off the candidate, but to give a serious honest answer to their question.

When you show that you are interested in them, they will begin to show an interest in you.

Many people are afraid that they do not have all the answers about Rotary or that the prospect will ask a question they cannot answer. It is always good to say that you don't know the answer, but that you will find out and get back to them. A simple call to your club president or assistant governor will find the answer. Then you can call your prospect back with the answer. It will impress them that you cared enough to spend the time to find the answer to their question.

It is a good idea to hold a fireside session and invite the new member's spouse or partner to this event. At this meeting you will be explaining the Rotary language that confuses most new members. Things like

PDG, RYE, RYLA, PETS, all need to be explained so that your new members and their families feel connected with the club.

Most of us want to recruit new members, but we simply don't know how or we just fail to think about it at the right time. I like to think that we fail to "focus" on recruiting. I say that because each of us sees about a dozen potential members every day. You go into the super market, the bank, the shoe repair shop or your dentist. We do all these tasks or maybe they are on our "honey-do " lists. We are simply getting the job done and probably we are warm and friendly to the people we meet. But we fail to see them as potential members.

When is the last time you thought about asking your banker or super market manager to consider joining your club?

You see these same people regularly, but when we discuss recruiting, they don't seem to pop into your mind. That is because when you go into these businesses, you are not thinking membership. You also don't have a club brochure in your pocket or purse. You don't have that little card inviting the person to be your guest for lunch or breakfast. Remember when your club had those printed and gave you a stack of them?

It would be a good exercise during a meeting to have each member think of three or four people that they might give those cards to and ask to be their guest at an upcoming meeting.

It is important to think of inviting someone to be your guest for a meal at your club. It is much better to invite them to share a meal than to invite them to a meeting. Most of us have way too many meetings to attend. But to share a meal with a friend, even a brand new one, is more interesting. It puts little pressure on the person to accept.

I find that if I over push the club message at that first meeting, it's not as effective as going light with the sales pitch. They are usually impressed with all that the club represents after they meet my fellow club members.

I do mention a project that we are doing to help our local community. I might focus on helping kids if the person is younger or I might talk about our senior care projects if they are older.

You gather personal information as you listen to them talk about what their interests are. We might take a good look at our club first. You are asking new members to join, so what would be the attraction for them? Do you have strong fellowship, an outstanding venue, a program of interesting speakers, meaningful hands-on projects? Do you meet at a convenient time?

These are important questions to consider. I usually let my potential guest know that the club meets at the local country club and that we meet from 8 - 9

am. It is important in my case to let them know that
we meet early, but not at 6 or 7. I tease that we meet
at a civilized time, 8 am. It is also important to let
them know that we only meet for one hour since that
tells them that they can plan their day around it.

Attracting is such a simple process, but so complex
for some members to understand. It is simply a matter of asking another person to attend a meeting.

I tend to invite the prospect to be my guest for breakfast and do not assume that they will join the club.
We do not even know if we want them to join at that
point. There may be a number of issues that would
make them not a good fit with the club. At times they
might have the wrong motivation for joining the Club.
We had a woman a few years ago whose motivation
was to sell jewelry to our members and she was very
clear about that right from the start. It was lucky for
the club that we sensed it before asking her to join.
But the reality is that most Rotarians in your club
have never asked anyone to join Rotary. According
to Rotary International, most Rotarians

(82% based on latest RI survey) never propose a new member.

It is important for you to carry a membership application in your coat or purse at all times. A business card with a personal invitation on the back of it would be helpful too. You might put a label on the back of your professional business card. The label will invite them to whatever meal your club holds as its meeting.

 Always know who the speaker is for your next meeting. It makes sense to invite your guest to gain knowledge or fun at the next meeting. Remember to check to see if your profession allows you to add that label on your business card. Certain professions such as financial planners may be restricted from adding a Rotary logo to the back of their business cards. By the way, you are not allowed to put a Rotary logo on your business card since it indicates an endorsement of Rotary by your company. This is a Rotary regulation.

Let's Get Those Baby Boomers!

Building membership has always been a challenge. Today, however, that challenge has become an opportunity, something very different from what it was in the past, because your focus might involve recruiting those who grew up during the Baby Boom era.

For the next two or three decades, this will be the generation that in large part will have the time and resources for significant contributions to Rotary.

We need to recruit in a way that truly engages the boomer audience, in a way that captures their attention and speaks directly to their wants, their interests, and their aspirations. Boomers are already volunteering at a higher rate than society at large with more than 60% of all boomers volunteering.

Boomers love to work in teams and Rotary follows that direction with its projects. Boomers are sensitive to feedback and driven by a sense of self-achievement.

74% of Rotarians are over 50 years old. So the average club already has a number of Baby Boomers. Many Boomers are not planning to retire on a full-time basis. Many Boomers consider themselves in a new and extended mid-life phrase. If they plan retirement, it might come more gradually or it might involve starting another business.

Ken Dychtwald's primary area of study has been the Boomer Generation and he tells us that many Boomers have "grown up equating retirement with old age, but with Boomers reaching sixty-five they aren't looking to be old or to wind down."

AARP CEO Bill Novelli tells us "there are more people starting their own businesses in this country who are over fifty than under fifty." We know that Boomers are not going to fade softly into the night. They are active, healthy and they expect to live to ninety and beyond.

Many Boomers are moving from a focus on money to a focus on meaning. It is this focus on meaning that will ignite the spirit of Rotary in the hearts of many Boomers. They are not going to be happy with many of the typical volunteer assignments usually assigned to senior citizens. They do not plan to roll carts loaded with magazines from hospital rooms to hospital rooms or serve apple juice to pre-schoolers.

Boomers have been activists and professional all their lives and they will not be planning to conduct them in any other fashion.

Boomers traditionally have a poor reputation for their rate of volunteering and for their involvement in other forms of civic life. Yet nearly a third of all Boomers — comprising some 25.8 million people — volunteer for formal organizations. These Boomers have the highest volunteer rate of any age group. The volunteer rate for Boomers — 33.2% — is the highest of any age group, and more than four percentage points above the national average of 29%.

Although most Americans, including Boomers, volunteer for only one organization, Boomers are the most likely of all age groups to volunteer for more than one organization. That may indicate that Boomers can be attracted to volunteering in several capacities.

This is good news for Rotary clubs since most volunteers, if they are at one organization will not offer their volunteer services to another organization.

It also appears according to the research from the *Corporation for National and Community Service* that strong community ties will play in areas such as community development and school reform. This might indicate that Boomer Rotarians will be interested in community service and youth programs.

The Corporation also states that Boomers who own businesses and are homeowners have higher volunteer rates — 45% and 34%, respectively — than do non-business owners and non-homeowners, who have average volunteering rates of 30% and 20%, respectively. Since most Rotarians are both business people and homeowners it looks good for our connection with Boomers.

One of the concerns we hear from Boomers is that they want to do meaningful work.

They want to use their professional talents and skills, rather than stuffing envelopes, answering phones and donating food.

Here's some evidence backing up my contention that Boomers like providing meaningful assistance when they volunteer. According to Richard Eisenberg in *Forbes Magazine*, "providing professional or management assistance, including serving on a board or committee" is the second most popular form of volunteering for Americans over 55, after "collecting, preparing, distributing or serving food."

Boomers are attractive volunteers, and it's not just the strength of their numbers — 77 million. They are living longer. They are more educated than previous generations.

Especially appealing, Boomers bring well-honed skills and years of work and life experience.
"What we have with the transition of the Boomers across the traditional age of retirement is a great opportunity," says Dr. Erwin Tan, who heads the *Senior Corps* program at the *Corporation for National and Community Service*, a federal agency in Washington.

The entire generation of Boomers is now between the ages of 45 and 65, prime ages for Rotary membership. It is very interesting that Boomer women volunteer at a higher rate than Boomer men. Approximately 36.9% of Boomer women volunteer, compared to 29.4% of Boomer men.

Attracting the Boomer is critical since the eldest are just now coming up on retirement.

Remember that this group doesn't see themselves slowing down, as they get older.

Many Boomers will be just as active as before, but they will be looking to replace their old jobs with a cause they are passionate about. This is great news for your Rotary club.

The *MetLife Foundation/Civic Ventures* "New Face of Work" Survey found that boomers have a strong desire to launch a new chapter in their working lives that involves significant social contribution. People over 50 showed a surprisingly high level of interest in making shifts from their intense midlife careers to new pursuits that improve lives in their communities.

This study tells us that "the Boomer generation is known for wanting choice, and every study to date has found that Boomers are not looking for busy work. They are looking for meaning and purpose.

They are looking for interesting and challenging opportunities to make an impact on big societal problems, from education to the environment, hunger to homelessness to health care." Does this sound like the vision and goals of your Rotary club?

Volunteer Match commissioned Peter D. Hart Research Associates to conduct a comparative analysis of the attitudes and experiences of individuals of all ages sampled from *Volunteer Match's* active user base.

The results are interesting for Rotary clubs. The research stressed that Boomers are having a more difficult time finding volunteer opportunities that interest them and compared to the general population. These boomers were noticeably more interested in making use of their existing skills and interests.

The following four research findings from this study are very interesting to us as we consider asking Boomers to consider Rotary.

1. Many Boomers are reconsidering volunteering and retirement as a time to begin a new chapter.

2. More than half of the Boomers report some interest in volunteering and professionals and women aged 55-64 are the most likely to be interested.

3. Many Boomers aren't volunteering because they haven't found the right opportunity.

4. Many Boomers are particularly interested in learning new skills and exploring new interests.

As you review these findings from this study I believe you will see that boomers are interested what Rotary has to offer so long as we help them find the right service projects based on their personal skills and talents.

We have a boomer in my club who was always thinking about a project, but never quite connected with any of them. That is until our Interact club considered starting a community garden. This individual's background is in parks and recreation and he jumped onto this project with both feet. He starting working with the Interact club and is now the chair of our very successful community garden that donates them to the food bank.

Dan Kadlec, writing in *Time Magazine* says, "the days of volunteers stuffing envelopes may be numbered." He accuses established nonprofits of clinging to "their old ways of asking volunteers to do little more than stuff envelopes and make fundraising call as a waste of talent and desire." We must be very careful in Rotary that we give these boomers, many of which retired as top leaders in their careers, meaningful tasks to take on.

The danger is that otherwise these boomers will get insulted and leave the organization.

These boomers are going to look for something meaningful to invest in for the next thirty years of their lives. They may not want another full time career and many, if not most of them are in good financial ways.

They will be looking for something that respects their skills and recognizes their talent pool. This is the perfect place for Rotary to place these boomers into solid leadership roles.

This period between mid-fifties and mid-eighties is going to be a period of great productivity for Boomers.

Boomers are looking for a feeling of worth, of giving back, of making a contribution.

This is a place where Rotary can gain from this audience and using quality leadership and recognition they will gain high quality membership and begin to fill the pipeline of Rotary membership.

Richard Croker in *The Boomer Century* says that Boomers are in a unique position. Croker says, "I don't think there's ever been a generation before that's reached this point in their lives, where they've had enough experience to know what they cared about, what they wanted, and enough time to do something with that experience."

In his book *Generation Ageless*, J. Walker Smith tells us that "as Boomers look ahead, two things are uppermost in their minds: endurance and impact."

It appears that for these Boomers to make that impact they will have to have a presence and an influence. This certainly sounds like Rotary, which has always involved the movers and shakers in any community. And it certainly has always made its presence felt and been an influence in all communities.

Boomers are a natural for an organization like Rotary, since their hopes, dreams, and aspirations for the next stage of their lives are grounded in a sense of self that revolves around moral causes and principles.

For Rotarians, the Four-Way Test is the cornerstone of all action. It has been the cornerstone for all Rotarians. This test is one of the hallmarks of Rotary and is a simple checklist for ethical behavior.

Once the Boomer finds this test, it will be hard to keep them out of the club. It is this righteous self that will become the dominant self. Baby Boomers are going to repurpose their lives and everything they do will likely be framed as a moral issue.

It is for certain that boomers will not leave the workplace to settle into an easy chair for the next thirty years.

They will be finding an active engaged life. It is interesting to note that our 2013-14 Rotary President Ron Burton's theme is *Engage Rotary, Change Lives.* He says that we will do that "by engaging Rotarians – by getting them involved, by getting them inspired, and by making sure that all Rotarians know just what a gift they have in Rotary."

He says that this goal is not just bringing in more members, but with more involved, engaged, motivated members who will be the ones to lead us into the future.

It seems clear that he is talking to Boomers as they move into retirement and finding opportunities for that second lifetime that Bob Buford tells as about in his book *Finishing Well.*

Buford says that for years he had been asking people, "Would you like the world to be a better place for your having been here?" Bob says everyone is quick to say "Yes!" But when he asked them what their plan is, they smile and laugh because they don't have one.

Buford in his prior book *Halftime* suggested that most Boomers would like to move from success to significance.

This is moving from the time in life when they felt they had to prove themselves to a time when they can give back and make a difference.

In the old times, whenever that was, they thought of those years past 60 as the start of the end of life. Then they got healthy, started to eat better and maybe even visit the gym sometimes.

But now they realize that they are still in that age when they can say that today's sixty is yesterdays forty. But even though they may be retiring and ready to travel and play golf, something is giving them second thoughts.

Many of the Boomers do not attend the senior center meetings or that church program for those over 50. They are not ready to be where their parents were at age 60. If you ask most of them how many want to be called seniors, I would venture a guess that it would be a very small number.

But most Boomers are looking to fill that void that comes after the success period of their life is closing and that significance period is looking for them. I believe that for Boomers, Rotary is a perfect way to move from their successful business career to a meaningful sense of significance.

Peter Drucker, at age 92 said "the goal is not just long life or even a prosperous one; it's to make a meaningful life out of an ordinary one."

I guess all of us wonder how we move after retirement to a significant life. Many of us ask ourselves, "What do I do now?" I think we all want to do some thing that literally makes a difference in the world.

Maybe that is to eliminate polio, stop babies from dying because of dirty water, or help establish the first neonatal cardiac surgery department in Ukraine. To all of us Rotarians it is not enough to think about what we can do, its not good intentions, we want to use our expertise, our knowledge, and our discipline to get the job done.

One Key Attraction Tool is Web 2.0

Web 2.0 is the term given to describe a second generation of the World Wide Web that is focused on the ability for people to collaborate and share information online. This indicates that Web 2.0 is a two-way exchange of information.

While Boomers were using the Internet to view web pages, the younger folks were using the web to communicate with their peers. Their online experience was the beginning of Web 2.0, a totally new method of communications.

Seventy one percent of all adults are online.

Most children are surfing the web today before they learn to ride a bike.

Dr. Idit Harel says "technology is completely transparent to kids and they don't talk about technology, they talk about playing, building a web site, writing a friend about the rain forest." The technology is completely transparent to them.

Today even most club members are texting and using social networks on a daily basis. Rotary clubs need to catch up with these new Web 2.0 tools. These are a number of social tools, not just the Internet.

We live in a massively connected world with over one billion people connected to the Internet.

More than 50 percent of US citizens have broadband access and these numbers increase daily. The key to Web 2.0 is its ability to be more participatory than the earlier Web 1.0 technologies.

We will rely a lot more on users generating and sharing content with each other. We are starting to see that everything we do online is going to have a social networking component. This social networking is an emerging phenomenon and will continue to develop in the years ahead.

In Lynne Lancaster's 2010 book, *The M-factor*, she tells us that, *"Many clubs do themselves a disservice by failing to let people know about the great work they do in making the world a better place."*

 She says that we should make sure that our web sites, print materials, and even those members recruiting emphasize our contributions to society. Lynne states that *" it's not only Ok to brag, it can be hugely rewarding."*

People are ready to hear Rotary's stories and it can create valuable social capital with prospective Rotarians as well as with the communities in which we do our volunteer work.

You might ask why social media matters. Just take a look at these numbers.

•57% of all adults has a social media profile.

•50% of all social networkers check their sites every day.

•Twitter use is growing at 400% per year.

•Facebook is the #2 destination on the web.

•The Average Facebook user has 120 friends.

•Over 850 million photos are updated to Facebook each month.

These are numbers that you can't ignore in your Rotary club. Rotary International has developed a presence on Facebook, Twitter, LinkedIn, Flickr, and YouTube.

Rotary clubs also need that presence online. It might be blogging, a Facebook business page or a club Twitter account.

For young people in particular, the most profound change is the pervasive connectedness of this new world. This is the constant connection to friends and even business peers. Clubs need to learn to search, share, and interact in this new connected way. The key to attracting people into Rotary is getting the word out in a form that will interest them.

Social media can help your club in a few areas of marketing. First is building relationships with both club members and prospects looking to learn more about Rotary.

Second is building the Rotary brand, and maybe just as important is building your club brand.

Public image enhancement comes from any brand building and it is a primary focus of Rotary International these days.

And third it is a great method for building awareness of your upcoming social and fundraising events.

In Paul Kiser's blog He made a number of interesting comments that clubs certainly should think about. He stresses the fact that for over thirty years clubs have relied on the club newsletter as the tool of connection and communication.

But today, Paul says "a newsletter is only slightly higher on the value scale than junk mail."

The problem he states is that few people have time to spend 15 minutes reading it and much of the information is not of interest to the reader. Enter Facebook and Twitter.

Paul tells us that most of the clubs that he has been involved with regarding Facebook or Twitter have included the statement that most of their club members don't use Facebook."

If there is a defining remark about the state of a club's attraction that is it.

Kiser states "over 500 million people use Facebook and Rotary clubs don't think it is relevant because their current members don't use it. If your members are not using the most current methods of communication that should tell you why people see your club as out-of-date and out of touch.

The club that doesn't have an active website, and a Facebook Page or twitter account will most likely be the club that is consistently struggling to maintain membership. It's that simple.

Paul Harris began Rotary to make connections with other people, I think Paul Harris would have loved Social Media.

Most of us know online social networking is a big deal, but don't know what to do about it. A few of us use Facebook in our personal lives but aren't quite sure how it fits with Rotary.

Just spend a few minutes and Google *Rotary social networking* and you will find the Official Rotary International Facebook page, the official Rotary blog, Rotary Voices, Rotary Google+, the Rotary Twitter page, the Rotary Linkedin page, the Rotary Flickr group pool, and the Rotary YouTube channel.

If you are not yet up to speed on all these social networking tools, it is time to start exploring them. In the January 2013 issue of *Rotary Leader* is an article on how to maximize your online presence. It suggests that each club plan a simple one-page digital strategy to help focus their goals. It suggests a website first, followed by a Facebook and Linkedin page.

There's even a Rotary Fellowship aimed at building friendships and support service through safe and effective social networking. During the 2009 RI Convention in Birmingham, England, a group of Rotarians interested in social media met to discuss forming a fellowship.

Recognized by the RI Board in June, *The Rotarians on Social networks Fellowship* has grown from an initial 488 members to almost 970 in 79 countries. "Members offer advice on how to determine goals for developing a presence on a social network, and how to best achieve those goals," said Simone Carot Collins, president of the Fellowship and of the Rotary Club of Freshwater Bay, Western Australia.

The mission of the fellowship is to promote Rotary fellowship, service and public relations utilizing all the tools available on social networks. On the ROSNF home page they explain that they are not just a website and what sets them about from other computer-based fellowships and Rotary-related groups and pages is that they provide comprehensive education and practical training and support about social networking for all levels of experience. If you are ready to jump into the social media arena, this might just be the place to visit on the web. This is certainly an outstanding version of a Web 2.0 site.

If you do not understand social media and you have kids, just go down the hall and watch them for a while. If you don't have kids of your own, spend some time with a friend's kids. Watch them playing, communicating, and learning. Notice how much of their lives are being spent on line.

Just visit an Apple store to watch the little ones play with technology.

According to Clara Shih in her book, *The Facebook Era*, "Thanks to their viral nature, we have reached the tipping point in the mass adoption of online social networks, and they will only continue growing in prominence and pervasiveness.

According to Facebook, although it maintains an 85 percent or greater penetration among four-year U.S. universities, more than half of its users are out of college, and those 35 and older represent the fastest-growing demographic.

Winogread in his book *Millennial Makeover*, tells us "younger voters are twice as likely as others to use the net, rather than the newspapers, to get information about political campaigns."

The most recent US Presidential election demonstrated the use of social networking sites as a political recruiting tool. We can learn a great deal from Barack Obama's 2008 presidential campaign, which used Facebook and other social networking sites to rally millions of supporters and helped raise nearly $1 billion in grassroots campaign contributions. By the time Obama officially announced his candidacy six months later, it had already accumulated over 50,000 members and would eventually attract over 250,000 members.

Did you notice that I said attracted? That is exactly how social media works, it attracts. You do not recruit members into your social media site, you attract them.

In Tom Heads book, *It's Your World, So Change It*, he speaks of social media like online dating. He says,

"You get on it to meet and interact with other people."

You may hear about a website through Google, but you hear about social networking sites through friends.

Your Facebook page gives your club a sense of community where members and friends find your updates concerning programs and events. Facebook gives you an area to promote events online, giving everyone the opportunity to receive invitations to specific events.

If the Xers and Millennial are the connected generation, then Rotary needs to become the connected club. Rotary International has joined this connected era with its social networking sites.

The Rotary International website says it best when it states, "Rotarians help provide service through fellowship, and social networking is one of the many ways Rotarians are connecting online."

According to the *Cone Study*, the bottom line is that the best way for organizations to reach young people with cause-related messages is to redefine the marketing experience. This study found that when a cause message is linked to a brand in an authentic and relevant way, it could gain the attention and respect of young people today.

Furthermore, a shared passion for a cause can foster a strong personal relationship between a brand and its target consumer. Younger adults are ready to reward or punish an organization depending on its commitment to social and/or environmental causes.

Cause marketing should be considered as a loyalty strategy for engaging them. The result of this study appears to suggest that young members will foster a strong relationship with Rotary only if they feel strongly about the service projects that the club is undertaking.

In fact, according to the study if they do not agree with the cause, they will likely fail to support the club based on their personal feelings. That makes it critical that we find those causes that today's young adults in fact are willing to support.

Too many clubs feel that once they put together a website, complete with an array of photos and maybe even a video clip or two that they are in the social media arena. Too many clubs simply scanned their brochures and put them up on their web page, but this barely scratches the surface of what this change in the digital landscape is all about.

For example a blog is not just another form of advertising your club's activities. *Blogger.com* says that a blog "is a personal diary, a daily pulpit, a collabora

tive space, a political soapbox, a breaking-news out-
let, a collection of links, your own private thoughts,
or memos to the world."

They tell us that a blog is whatever you want it to be.
There are millions of them, in all shapes and sizes,
and there are no real rules. In simple terms, a blog is
a web site, where you write stuff on an ongoing basis.
New stuff shows up at the top, so your visitors can
read what's new. Then they comment on it or link to
it or email you.

This idea of personal interaction means it is not a
corporate message, but it is opinions of individual
Rotarians being shared around the world. This is the
beauty of the social networks as they are akin to public spaces where Rotarians hang out.

It is important to realize that while these Web 2.0
technologies are inexpensive compared to the older
advertising methods such as buying space in a magazine or producing a television program, they will require time and learning.

They are not magic! You will have to spend time and limited resources to make them work.

But the connection you can gain with any of the social media tools is amazing.

Only a year ago I started my *Facebook.com/ RotaryMembership* blog and have been amazed at the response it has received. Just posting to it once a week allows over 2,000 people to view it and leave comments on it. The viewers are Rotarians and friends of Rotary from all over the world and many of the comments are in their native language.

Rotary Voices is the official blog for members of Rotary International. This blog features stories by and about Rotarians and Rotary program alumni about the humanitarian service projects they are involved with all over the world.

Paul Krauska's blog *Innovate Rotary!* is a fun and meaningful discourse on Rotary. His blog offers his personal opinions about Rotary and that is the real value of reading it on a regular basis.

A recent blog post "Nope, new clubs are not the path to growth" is a good example of Paul reviewing an article from *The Rotarian* magazine and adding his own opinions to the conversation.

The value of a blog depends on the content you publish.

The downside of a blog is that it takes effort to keep writing new entries and if you are not consistent it goes out of date fast. It's not as bad as a website that is out of date since the website tells the world about your meeting programs and activities, while the blog covers opinions and thoughts of the writer.

A blog is much less likely to date itself and will carry value for months, if not years. But like all social media, don't build any that you cannot maintain. It will frustrate many people but especially those younger people you are trying so hard to attract.

I am suggesting that your club put together a social media team to work on digital communication. Maybe the club trainer and/or the secretary might be the place to start, but it will require someone with the passion for Web 2.0 to keep this process alive and well.

> ## "I find it amazing and frustrating that so many club websites and Facebook pages have not had a new posting for months."

Antoinette Tuscano, senior supervisor for all of RI social media shares with us his thoughts about his use of the various social media applications.

"I've learned a lot from Rotarians about what's important to them in their communities, and several Rotarians have told me that social media has helped them feel the global reach of an organization that is so much more than their local Rotary club."

A Few Closing Thoughts

I hope I have made it clear that all service clubs are facing the fact that membership is falling and that younger people are not showing up to join. I guess we can blame lots of things for this decline in membership; the economy, generational differences, workplace pressures, family needs, to name just a few.

But it also seems that Rotary clubs need to assume some of the blame themselves. We have discussed many areas where change might help to fill this short fall in membership.

But I think we all realize that many members simply are not going into the community and asking anyone to be a guest at their club.

We also now realize that this loss of new members combined with the normal loss of existing members are causing many clubs to shrink to a smaller size.

Smaller clubs can be very strong clubs, but without a large enough membership your community service projects might be limited. Simply, more hands equals more work accomplished.

The worse part of this membership problem is that it appears that some clubs either don't care that they are getting smaller or are simply not aware of it.

Either way it becomes a membership issue.

It is time to stop recruiting and it's time to start attracting new members.

If people do not know the value of a Rotary membership or if they don't even know the club exists, then how do we get them to join.

Attraction is the best way to help potential members see the value of becoming a Rotarian. It will take the same marketing that helps all businesses sell more products or gather donations for a worthy cause.

It can be done with no or low cost social media tools. The good news is that these tools such as Facebook and Twitter will work equally with our younger or Boomer generation.

Maybe it's time to stop talking about the differences in generations, or stop talking about generational stereotypes. In many clubs I hear this common complaint from members. "They just don't get it." I know they are talking about the issues occurring between generations in the club.

Many of the club members want to increase the size of their clubs, but they are not sure how to do it or even who should do it. They don't like the conversations about change that come up when we talk about the younger generations. Remember what we said earlier, change is scary and frustrating.

The following two posts on the Rotary Membership blog on Facebook brings this to light. The post talked about the need for a club to consider changes first comment by Rotarian Robert Steinberg illustrates one viewpoint.

"Ah, but is it change we need to focus on? I don't think so. We need to do a better job of attracting people who would make great Rotarians. Of course, if you want to focus on a demographic who has little free time and little discretionary spending ability, then we would need big changes that would most likely drive out long time Rotarians. There are so many opinions about membership development, but most do not take into consideration the unintended consequences of upending Rotary!"

A follow-up post by Courtney Tyler takes a different viewpoint.

"as a young and very active Rotarian myself I thought I would offer my two cents, with all do respect of course. Small changes can go a long way for attract ing a younger demographic. My club has recently started encouraging evening service opportunities which has allowed more involvement from younger Rotarians. They also offer payment plans and make up opportunities for meetings. I feel these small changes are not intended to drive out long time Rotarians but to continue to allow clubs to thrive in a competitive service organization market. The 20/30 Club as well as young Chamber groups do not satisfy my personal need for community involvement and service towards others. We all have different circumstances and I enjoy the fact that Rotary is becoming inclusive for all age groups and genders. As for my "demographics" little free time and little discretionary spending ability.......I am 28 years old and I seem to manage my time just fine. I am actively involved in Rotary, my running group, my career with American Cancer Society, coaching underprivileged youth in health fitness programs at title one schools, and I manage to have a glass of wine now and then! Yes I have little free time but I assure you my demographic is in fact capable of scheduling wisely. I am also pretty good with my spending ability and although I have not had the years of experience to become promoted to higher paying positions within my industry, I do manage to pay my Rotary dues and sustaining membership just fine. Considering my current financial discretionary spending decisions, it may be in every Rotarians favor to encourage my "demographic" to support Rotary in the many years ahead. With that said, it is also in the younger generations favor to show respect and appreciation for the long time Rotarians who have paved the way to a thriving service club that gives back to so many communities. So, thank you Robert for paving the way and I hope you will guide and encourage my generation to understand the importance of service above self."

I think both Robert and Courtney are correct in their opinions. It is their opinion, neither right nor wrong. They simply represent two entirely different viewpoints concerning Rotary membership.

It would be worthwhile for every club to explore opinions like this. Sometimes veteran Rotarians will start joking about those offending generations of younger members. Then the younger members start talking about their club being "an old white man's club."

Each generation is attempting to maneuver others into seeing it their own way. They are trying to fix the other generation, rather than trying to under-stand generational differences. And then both sides are guilty.

The irony is that when we say another generation doesn't get it, we don't get it either. My hope is that you will learn how to attract, not recruit new Rotari-ans.

Our focus in this book has been on the two groups that I suggest you begin attracting into Rotary. That is the two younger generations and the Baby Boomer generation.

They are very different generations and while the
techniques of attraction may be similar, there are differences to consider. What works to attract the
younger group might be networking, social media
and lower cost environments, while the Boomers attraction might be increased fellowship, community
connections and the opportunity to do service. The
younger generation may need a few changes in the
club and the Boomers sort of fit right in with most
existing clubs.

The bottom line is clear. The younger generation
might require a little change and the older generation must embrace this change. Maybe at times we
need an interpreter to help to understand these issues to keep everyone on the same Rotary page.

We need to understand generational differences to
keep things from falling apart at times. At times neither generation understands the other generation
very well. It sometimes appears that we have two different countries housed in one Rotary club. But one
grew up in the 1940's and the other one in the 1980s.

They were taught differently in school, watched different events on TV and grew up in different neighborhoods. And these frustrations over small things in a club can lead members to start talking in stereotypes and that only makes things worse.

"It's stereotyping that can actually lead to some very negative outcomes and generalizations," said Steven Rogelberg, professor at UNC Charlotte. Stereotyping can be difficult in a club as we try to find ways to work together on projects.

We all know the labels. The Millennial lives their lives digitally. Gen Xers are cynical and not great team players, and Baby Boomers can't operate technology.

Can you find members who fit these stereotypes? Of course you can. Can you find people who smash them to pieces? I know we can in every Rotary club.

The truth is that people differ and it is our job to understands our members as individuals, not as members of a generation.

Maybe we need to stop wasting time blaming club issues on stereotypes and learn to appreciate the values in the generational differences sitting in those seats in your club.

So lets get started with our attracting teams and fire those recruiting committees.

As we said before in the words of Bob Dylan, "The times they are a changing."

 So lets get started changing!

If you would like to have Bill speak at one of your Rotary or association events, please contact him at:

Dr. Bill Wittich

8650 Heritage Hill Drive

Elk Grove, CA 95624

916-601-2485 cell

billwittich@comcast.net

www.volunteerpro.net

www.billwittich.com

www.facebook.com/rotarymembership

All of Dr. Wittich's books
are available in both
print and e-book formats.

They are available from
Amazon.com and Barnes & Noble.com

Kindle, Nook and Apple iPad
e-book formats
are available from the
Apple i-book store, Barnes & Noble.com and Amazon.com

Made in the USA
Monee, IL
12 September 2020